Gourmet Cooking The Slim Way

To Diane,

May these worldly recipes

Keep you slim

Lou Seibert Pappas

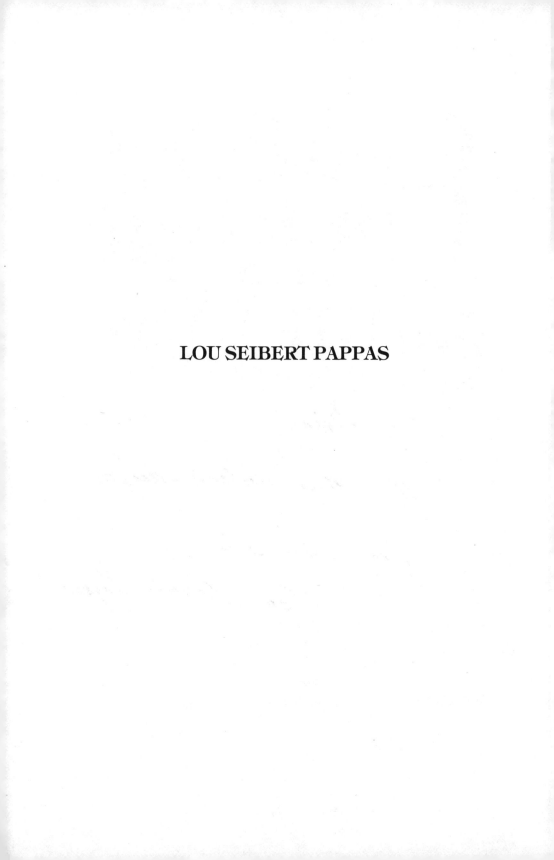

LOU SEIBERT PAPPAS

Gourmet Cooking The Slim Way

ADDISON-WESLEY PUBLISHING CO.
Reading, Massachusetts
Menlo Park, California • London
Amsterdam • Don Mills, Ontario • Sydney

Library of Congress Cataloging in Publication Data

Pappas, Lou Seibert.
    Gourmet cooking--the slim way.

    Includes index.
    1. Cookery, International. 2. Low-calorie
diet--Recipes. I. Title.
TX725.A1P29   641.5'635   76-57723
ISBN 0-201-05670-4
ISBN 0-201-05671-2 pbk.

Illustrations by Robert Rose

ISBN 0-201-05670-4-H
ISBN 0-201-05671-2-P

With love to Tamsen, Karen, and Andrea

Contents

Fish and Seafood / 71

Poultry / 87

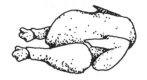

Meats / 99

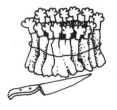

Vegetables / 135

Introduction

Here and abroad the trend is toward irresistible lighter food. Health is in the spotlight, and diet, the darling. This new food awareness is affecting almost everyone as counting calories and cholesterol shape today's life-style.

Simultaneously our desire for savoring international cuisines is spiraling. Increased travel sharpens palates to a worldwide sphere. Bounteous markets bring the ethnic and exotic foods to within easy reach. It is only logical to dovetail the slim and international cuisines. The result is a natural diet, delectably lean, celebrating the cuisines of the world.

Food for health is here, now. Choosing lower calorie ingredients and presenting nutritious food handsomely has become a way of life, even for those who do not need to tally calories. And for those who do, new guidelines have replaced tedious diet plans. The word diet stems from the Latin *diaeta* and Greek *diaita,* meaning "way of life" or "regimen." Today there is a new approach to the slim cuisine.

The focus is on a return to good fresh materials used in imaginative and experimental ways. The cook relies on the exquisite succulence of fresh fruits, vegetables, fish, and meats, preparing them to produce an eye-appealing dish that is simple, yet sophisticated. One is captivated by unexpected combinations, a counterpoint of flavors, and striking compositions. This philosophy readily suits the dynamics of contemporary life.

With a cosmopolitan menu pattern in vogue, its pleasures are infinite. New flavors can delight us at every meal. The diversity of dishes and combinations is endless; surprises are unlimited. A quest for the unique and different carries great momentum. And so we delve into cooking classes, pursue the latest cookware, seek out ethnic restaurants, and search for the specialty food shops.

My taste for what were then called foreign foods goes back to my Swedish and German heritage and a childhood nurtured in the Northwest Willamette Valley. Mother was a fine baker — a pro with whole-grain yeast breads and European tortes. My father managed a food co-operative at a university and daily provided the freshest from the marketplace. The household boasted a commercial-size Hobart Mixer which was constantly in use (for chores like) kneading bread dough, squeezing orange juice, blending mayonnaise, grinding round steak, shredding coleslaw, or churning ice cream.

After receiving a home economics-journalism degree from Oregon State University, I apprenticed at *Sunset Magazine* in California. My love for international dishes blossomed as I delved into varied cuisines developing articles. Later I married into a first-generation Greek family of superb cooks and discovered the Mediterranean ways of roasting meats and seasoning vegetables.

Since then, a succession of seven month-long European trips and several to Mexico have honed my enthusiasm for the international kitchen. I sought renowned delicatessens, colorful marketplaces, and diverse restaurants from the Finnish mainland to the Greek Isles. The recipes garnered readily adapt to the pace of the contemporary cook, and it is only sensible to streamline them to suit today's tastes. Whether you cook for one, or a family such as mine, with four children, the slim regimen makes sense.

The recipes here interweave to form charming world-wide menus for family or guests. Countless patterns are available with suggestions in the menu section. Dishes from several cultures also intertwine for a memorable meal. The result is a fascinating experience of international dining, styled with imagination, ease, and flair.

Portola Valley, California   *L.S.P.*
January 1977

A few guidelines help achieve a slim cuisine.

Sharpeners

Punctuate vegetables, salads, soups, and meats with shallots, a delicately flavored member of the onion family. • Utilize Dijon-style mustard to add piquant flavor to salad dressings and meat sauces. • Seek out fine wine vinegars, perhaps bottled with herbs, or flavor your own. • Peel garlic cloves, pack in a jar of olive oil, and refrigerate, ready for mincing and sprinkling on vegetables or lamb or lending zest to a salad dressing. • Add lemon juice, as the Greeks do, to bring out the natural flavors of meats, chicken, and vegetables as well as fish or seafood.

Lend zest with the grated peel of citrus fruits. • Fresh and dried herbs and spices are natural enhancers too. • Scatter a handful of chopped parsley over a salad, vegetable, fish, or meat to add flavor and color without calories. • Strew watercress, parsley, and even celery leaves around a platter in profusion for extra eye appeal. • Split a vanilla bean (a dried pod from certain orchids) and tuck in a jar of sugar or bottle of rum or brandy for lightly sweetening or scenting fresh fruits.

Secrets

Cornstarch yields a lighter, clearer sauce at one-fourth the impact of flour as it has twice the thickening power and half the calories, tablespoon per tablespoon. • Skim milk powder is a quick neat way to add protein and body (but few calories) to a sauce. • Sour half-and-half contains 30 calories per tablespoon as opposed to 50 for regular sour cream. • Buttermilk, cottage cheese, ricotta, and yogurt are fine bases for creamy types of salad dressings. • Don't forget the caloric bargains in vegetables: mushrooms contain only 64 calories in 1 pound and sugar peas contain 1 calorie apiece! • Try whipped margarines — they contain less fat.

Sauces

Low-Calorie Béarnaise Sauce

Instead of butter, yogurt and sour cream lend body to this smooth golden sauce for vegetables, fish, and meats.

1½ tablespoons each white-wine vinegar and dry Vermouth
sprig parsley
1 teaspoon chopped green onion
¼ teaspoon crumbled dried tarragon
2 egg yolks
½ teaspoon Dijon-style mustard
¼ cup low-fat yogurt
2 tablespoons sour cream

Combine in a saucepan the vinegar, Vermouth, parsley, onion, and tarragon; cook down until reduced to 2 teaspoons; let cool. Beat egg yolks with a whisk in the top of a double boiler and beat in mustard. Place over barely simmering water and let warm slightly, beating. Beat in strained vinegar glaze and 1 tablespoon yogurt, beating until blended. Add remaining yogurt and sour cream, 1 tablespoon at a time, beating until sauce is smooth and thick. Remove from heat. Makes ¾ cup sauce, or 4 to 6 servings. Total calorie count is 220 calories, or about 18 calories per tablespoon.

Yogurt Shallot Sauce

This piquant sauce enhances broiled fish or lamb patties or cooked green beans or spinach.

1 cup low-fat yogurt
2 shallots, finely chopped (about 3 tablespoons) or fresh chopped chives
2 tablespoons minced parsley
salt and pepper to taste

Mix together the yogurt, shallot, parsley, salt, and pepper. Cover and chill until serving time. Makes 1 cup sauce. Contains about 12 calories per tablespoon.

Yogurt Cilantro Sauce

In Middle Eastern fashion, cilantro sparks yogurt to spoon on sliced cold meats such as turkey, lamb, or beef, or broiled ground lamb patties.

½ cup low-fat yogurt
3 tablespoons chopped cilantro
¼ teaspoon ground cumin
¼ teaspoon garlic salt
dash Tabasco

Mix together the yogurt, cilantro, cumin, garlic salt, and Tabasco. Turn into a small bowl, cover, and chill. Contains about 12 calories per tablespoon.

Shopping Hints

- Filo dough is available in 1-pound packages in Greek markets and many delicatessens. Approximately 32 sheets come in each package, providing enough for several recipes.

- Cilantro, or fresh coriander, is a flat-leafed herb of the parsley family. It is available in Oriental and Mexican markets and now, increasingly, in supermarkets.

- Jicama and sun chokes are available in well-stocked produce departments.

- Sesame oil is found in various size bottles in Oriental markets.

Ethnic Menus

A Moroccan Safari Feast

Green Salad with Cucumber Dressing **61**
Veal and Apricot Tajine **104**
Crookneck with Herbs **141**
Crenshaw with Coriander **159**

A Greek Taverna Dinner

Greek Lemon Soup **39**
Salad Horiatika **63**
Moussaka **115**
Zucchini Orégano **153**
Apricot and Plum Basket

A French Country Dinner

Broccoli Bisque **44** or
Turkey and Veal Terrine **23**
Roast Chicken with Grapes **88**
Carrots Orangerie **140**
French Shallot Salad **56**
Strawberries in Wine **169**

An Oriental Guest Luncheon

Egg Flower Soup **48**
Tossed Shredded Chicken Salad **70**
Pineapple Boats **166**

An Italian Trattoria Supper

Caesar-style Salad **58**
Veal Scallopini with Marsala **125**
Green Beans Italian **142**
Zabaglione with Raspberries **168**

A Swedish Dinner

Spiced Orange Broth **36**
Swedish Style Cucumbers **62**
Veal Steaks Oscar **119**
Strawberry-Raspberry Bowls **156**

A Continental Luncheon

Onion Dip with Crudités **18**
Crab-Stuffed Artichokes **73**
Lemon Ice in Shells **175**

A Far East Repast

Crab-Stuffed Shrimp **17**
Snow Pea Soup **39**
Korean Steak Strips Teriyaki **109**
Asparagus Open Sesame **137**
Gingered Papaya with Lime **163**

A Burgundy Dinner

Leek and Potato Soup **43**
Steak and Mushrooms Dijon **103**
Asparagus with Low-Calorie Béarnaise **4**
Orange Crêpes Flambé **179**

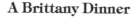

A Brittany Dinner

French Tomato Soup **46**
Soufflé-Topped Sole **81**
Shredded Zucchini **153**
Greens with Blue Cheese Dressing **62**
Caramelized Oranges **162**

A Roman Dinner

Fennel and Blue Cheese **15**
Beef Birds Spiedini **106**
Spinach-Stuffed Zucchini **151**
Tri-Color Salad **58**
Vanilla Bean Cheesecake **176**

An Istanbul Feast

Turkish Salad Tray **66**
Köfte **116**
Spinach and Mushroom Filo Roll **148**
Strawberries Laced with Pistachios and Cointreau **168**

An Athenian Dinner

Cheese Pitas **28**
Skewered Lamb Kebabs **132**
Artichokes Athena **139**
Sliced Tomatoes and Cucumbers
Basket of Pears and Grapes

An Amsterdam Spread

Egg and Anchovy Salad **65**
Dutch Cordon Bleu **101**
Green Pea and Spinach Soufflé **145**
Comice Pears with Candied Ginger **165**

A Cool Guadalajuara Supper

Mexican Tray Salad **68**
Mexican Steak Strips **21**
Papaya Honey Sherbet **164**

A Baltic Dinner

Borscht **35**
Veal Stroganoff **120**
Hot Green Beans or Spinach Soufflé **152**
Snow Peaches with Raspberry Sauce **162**

A Fjordland Picnic

Basket of Cherry Tomatoes
Yogurt Cheese **18**
Pickled Fish and Onion Rings **85**
Filbert Torte **177**
Nectarines or Peaches

A Florentine Guest Luncheon

Cannelloni-Style Crêpes **130**
Asparagus Vinaigrette Salad **57**
Apricots and Cheese Pyramid **158**

A Helsinki Luncheon

Sliced Tomatoes and Onion Rings
Asparagus and Eggs Scandinavian **78**
Raspberry Yogurt Parfait **170**

A Bavarian Dinner

Woodland Soup **40**
Roast with Shallot Sauce **106**
Spinach Soufflé **152**
Almond Dollar Wafers **178**
Fruit Basket of Nectarines, Peaches, and Plums

An Austrian Dinner

Spinach and Bacon Salad **60**
Veal and Mushroom Strudels **127**
Baked Tomatoes and Herbs
Salzburger Nockerls **176**

A Mediterranean Dinner

Cold Artichokes Piquant **138**
Veal Piccata **124**
Ratatouille **144**
Café Borgia **180**

A Mexican Fiesta Dinner

Avocado Shrimp Soup **33**
Fish Fillets Mexicali **83**
Steamed Zucchini and Crookneck
Melon Baskets **157**

A Hawaiian Dinner

Avocado Madrilène **33**
Skewered Swordfish **84**
Zucchini Orégano **153**
Pineapple Spears in Rum **156**

An Informal Provençal Dinner

Whaling Station Bouillabaisse **86**
French Shallot Salad **56**
Winter Pears and Brie

Appetizers and First Courses

"A little something to whet the appetite" is how the Greeks translate their word for *mezé*, or appetizers. And a savory little morsel is an apropos beginning for any party dinner. The French have their *hors d'oeuvres*, the Italians *antipasto,* the Russians *zakuski,* and the Danes *smørrebrød*. But there is no need for extravagance. One simple item, thoughtfully presented, is more welcome than a spread. Then your guests fully appreciate what follows.

This appetizer section is a potpourri of starters from many lands. At the hilltop Amalia Hotel in Delphi we exclaimed over the superb hot Spinach and Ricotta Pitas. The Hôtel de la Borda in Taxco serves a fiery version of the Mexican Steak Strips. A charming nosegay of *crudités* graced the yellow-checked cloth of a château country bistro. The Turkey and Veal Terrine is patterned after the tantalizing pâtés at Battendier in Paris. The Artichoke Frittata Squares are simplified versions of those sold at smart Milanese food shops, like Peck's. And the Crab-Stuffed Shrimp was the prelude to a recent Napa Valley wine country picnic.

Each appetizer can be a clue to the nationality of the menu that follows. Remember to consider the season. Papaya and Smoked Salmon are cooly refreshing in summer, while piping hot Cheese Pitas bring warmth to a mid-winter supper.

For an accompanying beverage, consider an imaginative dry white wine such as a California Sauvignon Blanc, White Zinfandel, Johannisberg Riesling, or Champagne; a French Muscadet or Pouilly-Fuisse; an Italian Soave; or an Alsatian or German Gewürztraminer. Or introduce Kir, a combination of Chablis and Cassis, a black currant liqueur. For this combine in a pitcher a bottle of Chablis and about ¼ cup of Cassis, choosing a good imported variety. Another delightful refreshment from Peré Bise in Talloires is framboise Champagne. To achieve this crush ⅓ cup fresh raspberries with 2 teaspoons sugar and let stand a few minutes for juices to exude. Then press berries through a wire strainer, discarding seeds. Spoon the raspberry juice into 4 or 5 chilled champagne glasses and pour in one fifth-size bottle of chilled Champagne.

Here are some appetizers you can assemble with a flourish.

Endive and Shrimp Boats

Spread the tip of endive leaves with curry-flavored yogurt and top with a tiny shrimp and sprig of dill or parsley.

Mushroom Caps and Clams

Fill mushroom caps with cottage cheese blended with canned minced clams and seasoned with minced garlic, freshly ground pepper, and chopped chives. Or fill caps with a mixture of cottage cheese and mashed blue or Gorgonzola cheese and sprinkle with minced parsley or chives.

Jicama Mexicali

Peel and slice jicama into 2-inch strips and serve with bowls of lime juice and coarse salt for dipping. Or sprinkle strips with Mexican seasoning and squeeze lime juice over all.

Celery and Caviar Sticks

Cut celery hearts into 2- or 3-inch sticks, leaving on the pretty plume of leaves, and spread each cavity with a thin layer of yogurt or cottage cheese. Then sprinkle with caviar.

Cucumber Slices with Salmon

Slice cucumbers about ¼-inch thick and garnish with a ribbon of smoked salmon or sardines and a sprig of dill.

Fennel and Blue Cheese

Slice fennel and spread with blue cheese mashed with yogurt.

Sun Chokes and Limes

Marinate sliced sun chokes (also called Jerusalem artichokes) in lime juice and sprinkle with herb salt or Mexican seasoning.

Melon or Pears with Proscuitto

Wrap chunks of crenshaw or cantaloupe melon or spears of fresh pears with proscuitto and spear with a toothpick.

Fresh Figs with Ham

Peel fresh white or black figs, wrap with a paper-thin slice of ham or proscuitto, and skewer with a toothpick.

Vegetable Skewers

Skewer cherry tomatoes, mushroom caps, and artichoke hearts on bamboo skewers and poke into a parsley-covered flower frog.

A Vegetable Nosegay

Arrange a festive basket of raw vegetables, or *crudités*, by placing a flower "frog" in a round wicker basket and using it to hold a "nosegay" of raw vegetables: a bunch of radishes, a cluster of sugar peas, a whole partially-sliced cucumber, asparagus spears, cherry tomatoes, mushrooms, tiny carrots, and zucchini sticks. Tuck parsley or romaine leaves between each vegetable so the basket won't look empty when the vegetables are gone.

Crab-Stuffed Shrimp

Pink, succulent shrimp sandwiched with fresh, flaked crab meat is the ultimate for an elegant appetizer or first course.

8 large cooked shrimp (about 12 shrimp to 1 pound)
2 tablespoons mayonnaise
1 tablespoon sour cream
2 teaspoons lemon juice
½ teaspoon grated lemon peel
2 teaspoons finely chopped parsley
¾ cup flaked Dungeness crab meat
watercress for garnish

Peel and devein shrimp and cut lengthwise almost, but not quite, in half. Mix together the mayonnaise, sour cream, lemon juice, lemon peel, and parsley. Mix in the crab meat. Spread crab filling inside the split shrimp and press together lightly. Cover and chill until serving time. Serve on a platter garnished with watercress. Makes 8 appetizer servings or 4 first-course servings. Contains 55 calories per stuffed shrimp.

Oysters in a Pocket

Slashed scarlet cherry tomatoes cradle smoke-enhanced oysters.

1 basket cherry tomatoes (about 12 ounces)
1 small can (3¾ ounces) smoked oysters
parsley

Wash tomatoes; then cut almost in half, not quite through. Slip an oyster inside and skewer with a toothpick. Arrange on a platter and garnish with parsley. Makes about 2 dozen appetizers. Contains about 10 calories per appetizer.

Yogurt Cheese

You can easily make a satiny cream cheese from yogurt. It is delicious plain with berries. Or mix it with chopped chives or tarragon and freshly ground pepper and spread it on mushroom caps or cherry tomatoes. It is a good low-calorie substitute for cream cheese.

1 pint low-fat yogurt
½ teaspoon salt
cheesecloth

Turn yogurt into a bowl and stir in the salt. Line a strainer or sieve with a double thickness of cheesecloth and suspend over a bowl. Spoon in the yogurt and tie the corners of cloth together. Let drain for 12 hours or overnight. Makes about ½ cup yogurt cheese. Contains about 250 calories, or about 30 calories per tablespoon.

Onion Dip with Crudités

This cool onion dip belongs with a basket or platter of raw relishes, arranged in a "nosegay" bouquet.

1 cup low-fat yogurt
1 cup sour half-and-half
1 envelope (1½ ounces) dry onion soup mix
relishes: cherry tomatoes, small mushrooms, zucchini or cucumber, cauliflower, red or green peppers, Belgian endive, and fennel or celery strips

Combine the yogurt, sour half-and-half, and dry soup mix, stirring well. Turn into a serving bowl, cover, and chill. Accompany with a basket or platter of chilled relishes. Makes about 2 cups. Contains about 24 calories per tablespoon of dip.

Chicken Liver Pâté

This smooth pâté has a rich, almost buttery taste, yet there's almost no butter in it.

4 green onions, chopped
½ teaspoon butter
½ pound chicken livers
1 tablespoon tarragon-flavored white-wine vinegar
½ teaspoon garlic salt
2 tablespoons cottage cheese
2 tablespoons parsley
2 teaspoons finely chopped pistachios or toasted filberts

Sauté onions in butter until glazed. Add chicken livers and cook until brown. Add vinegar and garlic salt; cover and simmer 5 minutes. Let cool. Purée in a blender with cheese and parsley. Turn into a crock, cover, and chill. If desired, sprinkle with nuts at serving time. Makes about 1¼ cups. Contains about 20 calories per tablespoon.

Papaya and Smoked Salmon

Fruit paired with smoked fish is a refreshing way to introduce a summer dinner.

1 large papaya
2 ounces smoked salmon
1 lime
watercress

Peel papaya, halve, scoop out seeds, and slice. Arrange several slices on each salad plate and drape with smoked salmon. (Or cube the papaya, wrap with a salmon strip, and skewer with a toothpick.) Garnish with a wedge of lime and watercress sprigs. Makes 4 servings. Contains about 60 calories per serving.

Steak Strips Tartar

A smothering of chopped mushrooms, onions, and red wine infuses steak strips as they chill, tenderizing and subtly "cooking" the meat.

1½ pounds top round steak, sliced into thin strips
⅓ cup parsley
wine and mushroom marinade: see below
watercress sprigs

Alternate layers of meat strips and parsley in a shallow baking dish or bowl. Pour over the hot Wine and Mushroom Marinade (see below). Cover and chill 2 days. To serve, arrange meat slices on a platter and spoon some of the marinade over it. Garnish with watercress. Serves 12 as an appetizer or 6 as an entrée. Contains about 100 calories per appetizer serving.

Wine and Mushroom Marinade: Finely chop 3 shallots or green onions (white part only) and sauté in 1 teaspoon olive oil until limp. Add ¼ cup red-wine vinegar, ¾ cup dry red wine, ½ teaspoon beef stock base, 2 cloves minced garlic, ¼ teaspoon crumbled dried thyme, and ¼ teaspoon each salt and pepper. Bring to a boil and let reduce slightly. Add ⅓ pound finely chopped mushrooms and simmer, covered, 2 minutes.

Mexican Steak Strips

This appetizer seasoned with cilantro and lime juice makes a choice entrée as well.

1 pound top round steak
½ teaspoon salt
1 teaspoon Mexican seasoning (or ¼ teaspoon each cumin, orégano, seasoned pepper, and garlic salt)
1 tablespoon olive oil
3 tablespoons water
2 tablespoons lime or lemon juice
1 clove garlic, minced
3 tablespoons chopped cilantro
6 small, canned red peppers or ¼ cup fresh, chopped, sweet red pepper for garnish
cilantro sprigs

Season meat with salt and Mexican seasoning and brown in 1 teaspoon of the oil, turning to brown both sides and cooking until medium rare. Transfer to a platter and chill. Pour water into pan and scrape up drippings. Pour into a bowl and reserve. Slice ⅛-inch thick and arrange on a platter. Mix together the pan juices, the remaining oil, lime juice, garlic, and cilantro and spoon over meat. Chill for 1 to 2 hours. Garnish with peppers and cilantro sprigs. Makes 4 entrée servings or 2 dozen appetizer servings. Contains 225 calories per entrée serving, or 40 per appetizer serving.

Country-Style Terrine

Thin ribbons of proscuitto form stripes through this spicy meat loaf.
Serve it chilled, like a pâté, so the seasonings penetrate it smoothly.

1 onion, chopped
1 teaspoon butter or nonstick pan
1 pound lean ground veal or calf
½ pound lean ground chuck or round
2 cloves garlic, minced
2 tablespoons brandy
1 teaspoon salt
½ teaspoon each thyme and allspice
¼ teaspoon each ground ginger, cloves, and pepper
2 eggs
3 tablespoons nonfat dry milk solids
4 slices proscuitto
3 tablespoons pine nuts or shelled pistachios
2 bay leaves
peppercorns

Sauté onion in butter, preferably, or in a nonstick pan, until tender; let
cool. Mix together ground meats, onion, garlic, brandy, salt, thyme,
allspice, ginger, cloves, pepper, eggs, and milk solids. Line a
4½-by-7-inch loaf pan with a layer of proscuitto and half the meat
mixture. Sprinkle with half the nuts. Cover with proscuitto, remaining
meat mixture, and nuts. Decorate with bay leaves and a few
peppercorns. Place in a pan of hot water and bake in a 350° oven for
1¼ to 1½ hours or until set. Makes 8 servings. Figure 185 calories
per serving.

Turkey and Veal Terrine

Ribboned with green herbs, this colorful pâté makes an exceptional first course or luncheon entrée. You might accompany it with marinated mushrooms, artichokes vinaigrette, or tiny French gerkins.

1 onion, finely chopped
½ teaspoon butter or nonstick pan
1 whole chicken breast, boned and thinly sliced
1 tablespoon brandy or Cognac
1½ teaspoons salt
¼ teaspoon each pepper and nutmeg
½ teaspoon each thyme, basil, allspice, and lemon peel
¾ pound each ground turkey and ground veal or calf
1 egg
2 egg whites
3 tablespoons nonfat dry milk solids
¼ cup chopped parsley
2 shallots, chopped
1 clove garlic, minced
2 bay leaves
peppercorns

Sauté onion in butter or in a nonstick pan until tender. Let chicken strips marinate in brandy with a light sprinkling of salt, pepper, and nutmeg. Mix remaining salt, pepper, and nutmeg with thyme, basil, allspice, and lemon peel. Combine the ground meats with onion, the spices, egg, one egg white, and milk solids. Spoon half the meat mixture into a buttered 4½-by-7-inch loaf pan. Mix parsley, shallots, garlic, and remaining egg white and spread over meat mixture. Cover with remaining meat mixture. Arrange chicken in a layer on top. Decorate with bay leaves and a few peppercorns. Cover with foil and bake in a 350° oven in a pan containing 1 inch hot water for 1¼ to 1½ hours or until set. Let cool and chill. Slice. Makes 8 to 10 servings. Contains 160 to 200 calories per serving.

Individual Terrines: As a variation, arrange the pâté mixture in 8 to 10 medium-sized muffin pans, and proceed as above, reducing baking time to 40 minutes.

Potted Herb Cheese

A crock of herb-flavored cheese makes a flavorful spread for assorted raw vegetables. Or spoon the cheese inside a bright red or green pepper shell or on top of a circle of orange slices for a salad plate.

1 cup low-fat, small-curd cottage cheese
⅓ cup low-fat yogurt
3 tablespoons each minced parsley and spinach
2 tablespoons minced shallots
¾ teaspoon crumbed dried tarragon or basil or 2 teaspoons chopped fresh basil
1 clove garlic, minced
dash Tabasco
salt and pepper to taste
assorted raw vegetables, such as mushroom caps, zucchini slices, cherry tomatoes, and celery or fennel sticks

Place in a blender container the cottage cheese, yogurt, parsley, spinach, shallots, tarragon, garlic, and Tabasco and blend until finely minced. Add salt and pepper to taste. Turn into a small crock, cover, and chill. Makes 1½ cups. Serve with a tray of assorted vegetables. Contains about 13 calories per tablespoon.

Eggplant Caviar

In the Middle East, this eggplant plays many roles — appetizer, relish, or salad. Romaine leaves or Arab bread serve as a "handle" to scoop it up.

1 large eggplant
3 tablespoons red- or white-wine vinegar
1 tablespoon olive oil
½ teaspoon salt
¼ teaspoon each cumin and ground pepper
⅛ teaspoon allspice
3 tablespoons chopped parsley
1 tomato, peeled and chopped
2 green onions, chopped
romaine leaves

Place eggplant in a shallow baking pan and bake in a 375° oven for 50 minutes or until soft. Dip in cold water and peel off skin. Dice and place in a bowl. Combine vinegar, oil, salt, cumin, pepper, and allspice and pour over eggplant, mixing well. Mix in parsley, tomato, and onions. Cover and chill at least 1 hour for flavors to blend. Spoon onto romaine leaves to serve as a salad. Makes 6 servings. Contains about 35 calories per serving.

Crab Pitas

Crab and cheese make a succulent filling for filo triangles. Freeze them before baking so you can serve them piping hot whenever you want.

8 ounces ricotta cheese
1 egg
2 tablespoons chopped parsley
2 green onions, chopped
1 teaspoon grated lemon peel
¼ teaspoon Worcestershire
dash Tabasco
¼ teaspoon salt
8 ounces Dungeness crab meat or small cooked shrimp
⅓ cup grated Parmesan cheese
12 sheets filo dough
4 tablespoons butter, melted

Mix together the ricotta, egg, parsley, onions, lemon peel, Worcestershire, Tabasco, salt, crab, and Parmesan. Lay out filo dough and cover with clear plastic wrap. Using one sheet at a time, brush lightly with butter. Cut into 6 strips, each about 3 inches wide. Place a teaspoonful of cheese filling at one end of each. Fold each strip like a flag and place seam side down on a greased baking sheet. Brush tops with melted butter. Bake in a 350° oven for 15 minutes or until golden brown. Makes about 6 dozen. Contains about 20 calories per serving.

Spinach and Ricotta Pitas

Spinach and cheese puffs inside flaky filo triangles making a hot appetizer that melts in your mouth.

1 bunch green onions, finely chopped
1 teaspoon safflower oil
1 bunch spinach, finely chopped (about 1 pound)
½ teaspoon garlic salt
8 ounces ricotta cheese
2 eggs
⅓ cup grated Parmesan cheese
salt and pepper to taste
12 sheets filo dough
4 tablespoons butter, melted

Sauté onions in oil until glazed. Add spinach and cook just until wilted; drain off extra juice. Add garlic salt and let cool. Mix together the ricotta, eggs, cheese, and spinach mixture. Season with salt and pepper to taste. Lay out filo dough and cover with clear plastic wrap. Using one sheet at a time, brush lightly with butter. Cut into 6 strips, each about 3 inches wide. Place a teaspoonful of cheese filling at one end of each. Fold each strip like a flag and place seam side down on a greased baking sheet. Brush tops with melted butter. Bake in a 350° oven for 15 minutes or until golden brown. Makes about 6 dozen. Contains about 20 calories per appetizer triangle.

Cheese Pitas

Three cheeses fill these delicate filo pastries.

1 pint (1 pound) low-fat cottage cheese
8 ounces ricotta cheese
2 ounces feta cheese
2 eggs
1 green onion, chopped
2 tablespoons minced parsley
12 sheets filo dough (approximately)
¼ cup melted butter

Beat together the cottage cheese, ricotta cheese, feta, eggs, onion, and parsley. Lay out the filo dough and cover with clear plastic wrap. Using one sheet at a time, brush very lightly with butter. Cut into 6 strips, each about 3 inches wide. Place a teaspoonful of cheese filling at one end of each. Fold each strip like a flag and place seam side down on a greased baking sheet. Brush tops with melted butter. (If desired, wrap and freeze at this point.) Bake in a 350° oven for 15 minutes or until golden brown. Makes about 6 dozen. Contains about 20 calories per appetizer serving.

Spinach and Onion Squares

Here is a versatile appetizer that works well as a vegetable dish instead. Cut it into diamonds for an appealing change.

2 bunches green onions, chopped
1½ teaspoons whipped margarine
1 large bunch spinach, chopped
½ cup finely chopped parsley
4 eggs
½ cup low-fat yogurt
½ teaspoon each salt and crumbled dried tarragon
¾ cup shredded Gruyère cheese

Using a large frying pan, sauté onions in margarine until limp. Add spinach and sauté 1 minute. Remove from heat and add parsley. Beat eggs until light and mix in yogurt, salt, tarragon, cheese, and the onion mixture. Pour into a lightly greased 9-by-13-inch pan. Bake in a 350° oven for 20 minutes or until set. Cut into squares and serve hot. Makes 9 servings as a vegetable dish or 16 appetizer squares. Contains 48 calories per appetizer or 85 calories per vegetable serving.

Artichoke Frittata Squares

The rich succulence of artichoke hearts belies their lean calorie count
in these appetizer squares that are good hot or cold.

2 packages (9 ounces) frozen artichoke hearts
3 tablespoons green onions, chopped
1 teaspoon whipped margarine
¼ cup chopped parsley
4 eggs
½ cup low-fat yogurt
½ teaspoon each salt and dried basil
¾ cup shredded Cheddar cheese
½ cup toasted French bread croutons

Cook artichokes in boiling salted water until crisp tender; drain and
chop. Sauté onions in margarine until limp; add artichokes and heat
through. Mix in parsley. Beat eggs until light and mix in yogurt, salt,
basil, artichoke mixture, cheese, and croutons. Turn into a buttered
9-inch square pan. Bake in a 350° oven for 20 minutes or until set. Cut
into squares and serve hot or cold. Makes 16 appetizer squares.
Contains about 50 calories per serving.

Soups

Soups are wonderfully nourishing and inexpensive. Offering an endless variety, they are appropriate for almost any meal of the day, no matter how formal. The spectrum includes blender breakfast soups, tantalizing first-course soups, vegetable luncheon soups, and hearty full-meal soups. All can be made in advance; in fact, their flavors mellow on chilling.

A charming way to introduce a party meal is to pass around a sippable first-course soup in the living room or the garden. You may use small mugs, Japanese tea cups, little Bavarian stoneware bowls, or small fluted soufflé dishes as containers. Spiced Orange Broth or Greek Lemon Soup are good starter soups. Or Jamaican Carrot Soup is always a success, whether hot or cold.

Vegetable soups such as Mushroom Bisque or Belgian Sprout Soup are perfect for luncheon with a salad alongside. (In these calorie-pared soups, the vegetable purées provide rich body and thickness. Buttermilk is another secret to creaminess.) These soups look regal in French copper ramekins with shiny brass handles. Such full-meal soups as Moroccan Meatball Soup or Whaling Station Bouillabaisse (in the Fish and Seafood section) make warming winter suppers. A green salad and Comice pears might complete the meal.

Avocado Shrimp Soup

Buttermilk lends an easy low-calorie base for a frosty cold soup. This one retains upon standing the beautiful hue of the avocado.

1 medium-sized avocado, peeled and halved
2 cups buttermilk
½ teaspoon garlic salt
1 green onion, chopped
¼ pound small cooked shrimp or 1 can (7 ½ ounces) minced clams, drained
yogurt
chopped chives or chopped green onion

Place in a blender container the avocado, buttermilk, garlic salt, and onion. Blend until smooth. Turn into a jar, cover, and chill. To serve, mix in shrimp or clams and pour into bowls or large-bowled wine glasses. Garnish with a dollop of yogurt and sprinkle with chives. Makes 4 servings. Contains about 150 calories per serving.

Avocado Madrilène

This exotic, quick to make soup is excellent for introducing a party meal on a warm day.

2 cans (10 ½ ounces) consommé, chilled
1 avocado
1 tablespoon lemon juice
3 tablespoons sour half-and-half
1 small jar (2 ounces) red caviar
1 tablespoon chopped chives or green onions

Turn chilled consommé into a bowl and mix with a fork to break up lightly. Peel and dice avocado and sprinkle with lemon juice to prevent darkening. Lightly mix avocado into the consommé and spoon into small soup bowls or tea cups. Top with a spoonful of sour half-and-half and caviar. Sprinkle with chives. Serve at once. Makes 8 servings. Contains about 80 calories per serving.

Gazpacho

This bright Spanish soup shines as a summer first course or luncheon entrée.

1 large cucumber
1 sweet red onion
4 tomatoes
3 cloves garlic, minced
1 cup condensed beef broth
2 cups V-8 vegetable juice
3 tablespoons white- or red-wine vinegar
dash Tabasco
1 teaspoon each salt and Mexican seasoning
condiments: diced avocado, chopped green onions, and croutons

Peel and chop cucumber, onion, and tomatoes. Place in a bowl and add garlic, beef broth, vegetable juice, vinegar, Tabasco, salt, and Mexican seasoning. Cover and chill. Serve in chilled bowls and pass condiments for guests to add. Makes 6 servings. Contains about 60 calories per serving, varying with condiments added.

Borscht

This renowned Russian soup is wonderfully wholesome. It makes a fine winter entrée to serve with little meatballs.

**3 beets, peeled
1 carrot, peeled
1 medium-sized onion, peeled
1 turnip, peeled
1 cup shredded red cabbage
1 tablespoon butter
1½ quarts beef stock
3 tablespoons red-wine vinegar
1 teaspoon brown sugar
salt and pepper to taste
2 tablespoons cornstarch blended with cold water
sour half-and-half or yogurt
lemon slices or chopped chives**

Finely shred the beets, carrot, onion, turnip, and cabbage. Using a large soup kettle, sauté vegetables in butter until glazed. Pour in beef stock and add vinegar, sugar, salt, and pepper. Cover and simmer 45 minutes. Blend in a paste of cornstarch and water and cook until thickened. Ladle into bowls and garnish with a spoonful of sour half-and-half or yogurt and lemon slices or chives. Makes 8 servings. Contains about 50 calories per serving.

Wine Broth with Pesto

A dollop of Italian pesto sauce lends a fragrant flourish to a sippable, burgundy-scented broth.

1 tablespoon butter
⅓ cup grated Parmesan cheese
1 clove garlic, minced
4 teaspoons finely chopped fresh basil (or 1 teaspoon dried basil)
2 teaspoons finely chopped parsley
3½ cups beef broth
¼ cup dry red wine

Mix together in a small bowl the butter, cheese, garlic, basil, and parsley. Heat broth and wine until steaming. Ladle into small bowls or cups and add a dollop of pesto sauce to each. Makes 6 servings. Contains about 65 calories per serving.

Spiced Orange Broth

Cinnamon and cloves spice this citrus broth.

1 quart rich beef broth
1 cup orange juice
6 whole cloves
1 small stick cinnamon
2 strips orange zest

Combine in a soup kettle the broth, orange juice, cloves, and cinnamon. Simmer 15 minutes for flavors to permeate. Cut zest into fine strips, about $1/16$ inch wide and ½ inch long, and add 1 tablespoon to the broth. Ladle into cups. Makes 8 servings. Contains about 20 calories per serving.

Chilled French Vegetable Soup

Here is a beautiful orange soup for a warm day.

1 large onion, chopped
2 green onions, chopped (white part only)
1 teaspoon butter
5 cups rich chicken broth
1 medium-sized turnip, peeled and diced
6 large carrots, peeled and diced
3 cloves garlic, minced
¼ teaspoon nutmeg
salt and white pepper to taste
yogurt for garnish

Using a large soup kettle, sauté onions in butter until glazed. Add broth, turnips, carrots, garlic, and nutmeg. Cover, bring to a boil, and simmer 20 minutes, or until vegetables are very tender. Whirl in a blender or force through a food mill until smooth. Season with salt and pepper to taste and, if necessary, thin to desired consistency with additional broth. Chill. Ladle into bowls and garnish with yogurt. Makes about 8 servings. Contains about 60 calories per serving.

Cold Cumin Crookneck Soup

This frosty golden yellow soup is an inviting hot-weather first course.

4 crookneck squash, trimmed and sliced (about 1½ pounds)
1 medium-sized carrot, peeled and sliced
1 large onion, chopped
1 leek, sliced (white part only)
2 cloves garlic, minced
3 cups chicken stock (or 3 cups water and 4 bouillon cubes)
¼ teaspoon ground cumin
⅛ teaspoon ground nutmeg
dash Tabasco
salt to taste
¼ cup low-fat yogurt
chopped chives or minced parsley

Place in a large saucepan the squash, carrot, onion, leek, garlic, chicken stock, cumin, and nutmeg. Cover and simmer 15 minutes. Add Tabasco, turn into a blender container, and purée. Add salt to taste. Chill. Serve with yogurt and chopped chives. Makes 6 servings. Contains 40 calories per serving.

Snow Pea Soup

Just a few ingredients floating in a broth make an enticing Oriental soup.

3 cups hot fish or chicken stock
dash Tabasco
12 edible pod peas
4 mushrooms, sliced
4 cooked, peeled medium shrimp

Heat stock to boiling, add Tabasco, peas, mushrooms, and shrimp and cook 2 minutes. Ladle into bowls. Makes 4 servings. Contains about 30 calories per serving.

Greek Lemon Soup

The Greek way of whisking lemon and eggs with broth results in a remarkable low-calorie, yet filling, soup.

1 quart chicken broth
2 tablespoons each cornstarch and cold water
4 eggs
¼ cup lemon juice
parsley sprigs

Heat chicken broth to boiling and stir in a paste of cornstarch and water. Cook 2 minutes. Whisk together eggs and lemon juice and pour half the broth into the egg mixture, whisking constantly. Return to saucepan and cook over very low heat, stirring constantly. Ladle into soup bowls or small Japanese tea cups or soufflé dishes and garnish with a parsley sprig. Makes 8 servings. Contains about 45 calories per serving.

Woodland Soup

This unusual mushroom and egg soup comes from a fine German cook.

2 shallots or green onions, finely chopped (white part only)
¼ pound mushrooms, sliced
2 teaspoons butter
1 quart chicken stock (homemade or canned)
¼ teaspoon crumbled dried tarragon
¼ cup dry white wine
1 large tomato, peeled and chopped
2 hard-cooked eggs, chopped
1 tablespoon chopped parsley

Using a heavy saucepan, sauté shallots and mushrooms in butter until glazed. Pour in stock, add tarragon and wine, and simmer 10 minutes. Just before serving stir in chopped tomatoes, eggs, and parsley. Ladle into soup bowls. Makes 4 luncheon-size servings or 6 to 8 pass-around first-course servings. Contains about 85 calories per luncheon-size serving.

Green Soup

A mélange of fresh green vegetables turns into a filling first-course or luncheon soup to serve with a pâté or cheese and fruit.

3 zucchini, sliced
1 bunch green onions, coarsely chopped
1 cup chopped celery leaves
¼ cup chopped parsley
3 tablespoons fresh basil, chopped, or 1 teaspoon dried basil
1 clove garlic, minced
2 potatoes, peeled and diced
3 cups water
6 chicken bouillon cubes
salt and pepper to taste
seasoning salt or paprika for garnish

Place in a large soup pot the zucchini, onions, celery leaves, parsley, basil, garlic, potatoes, water, bouillon cubes, salt, and dash of pepper. Cover and simmer 15 to 20 minutes or until vegetables are very tender. Let cool slightly and purée in a blender until smooth. Season with salt and pepper to taste. Reheat before serving and sprinkle with seasoning salt or paprika. Makes 6 servings. Contains 40 calories per serving.

Belgian Sprout Soup

A creamy purée of sprouts cooked in herb-seasoned stock makes a stimulating first course.

1 pound brussels sprouts
3 green onions, chopped
2 cups rich chicken stock or 2 cups water and 4 chicken bouillon cubes
½ teaspoon salt
dash white pepper and tarragon
¼ cup nonfat dry milk solids
2 tablespoons low-fat yogurt
1 tablespoon chopped parsley
yogurt or chopped parsley for garnish

Cook sprouts and onions in chicken stock with salt, pepper, and tarragon until tender, about 10 to 15 minutes. Purée in a blender with milk solids, yogurt, and parsley. Reheat until hot through. Garnish with a dollop of yogurt or parsley. Makes 4 servings. Contains about 65 calories per serving.

Leek and Potato Soup

This flavor-packed vegetable soup is fortifying for either lunch or dinner.

1 medium-sized onion, chopped
1 teaspoon olive oil or margarine
1 bunch leeks, washed and chopped
2 potatoes, peeled and diced
½ cup celery leaves
1 quart chicken broth
½ teaspoon salt
¼ teaspoon nutmeg
1 cup buttermilk
chopped chives or parsley for garnish

Using a large soup kettle, sauté onion in oil until limp. Add leeks, potatoes, celery leaves, chicken broth, salt, and nutmeg. Cover and simmer 15 minutes, or until potatoes are tender. Cool slightly, then purée in a blender. Mix in buttermilk and reheat until hot through. Ladle into bowls or mugs and sprinkle with chives or parsley. Makes 6 to 8 servings. Contains about 50 to 60 calories per serving.

Broccoli Bisque

Let this lightly curried cool soup start an Indian summer meal.

1 large bunch broccoli
3 cups chicken stock
1 medium-sized onion, quartered
1 teaspoon salt
2 teaspoons curry powder
2 tablespoons lime or lemon juice
8 lemon slices
¼ cup low-fat yogurt

Trim broccoli and cut into flowerets. Place in a large saucepan with chicken stock, onion, salt, and curry powder. Cover and simmer about 12 to 15 minutes, or until broccoli is tender. Let cool. Purée in a blender with lime juice. Chill. Serve in bowls garnished with lemon slices and a dollop of yogurt. Makes 8 servings. Contains about 50 calories per serving.

Buttermilk Soup

It takes only minutes to make this cold soup. Its thick consistency belies its slim calorie count.

1 quart buttermilk
½ teaspoon each salt and Worcestershire
3 drops Tabasco
1 tablespoon lemon juice
1 large cucumber, peeled and chopped
3 tablespoons each minced chives and parsley
½ cup small cooked shrimp
salad seasoning or seasoning salt

Mix together the buttermilk, salt, Worcestershire, Tabasco, lemon juice, cucumber, chives, parsley, and shrimp. Chill at least 1 hour. Ladle into soup bowls and sprinkle with seasoning salt. Makes 6 servings. Contains about 75 calories per serving.

Mushroom Bisque

A blender speeds the making of this creamy, herb-scented bisque.

1 medium-sized onion, chopped
1 tablespoon butter
½ pound mushrooms, chopped
3 tablespoons chopped parsley
1 quart chicken stock
1 clove garlic, minced
1 teaspoon salt
freshly ground pepper
½ teaspoon tarragon
⅓ cup nonfat dry milk solids
1 tablespoon cornstarch blended with 1 tablespoon cold water
2 tablespoons dry Sherry (optional)
sour half-and-half or yogurt
paprika or salad supreme seasoning

Using a soup kettle, sauté onion in butter until limp. Add mushrooms,
1 tablespoon parsley, chicken stock, garlic, salt, pepper, and tarragon.
Cover and simmer 5 minutes. Cool slightly, then purée in a blender
with milk solids, cornstarch paste, and remaining parsley. Reheat and
stir in Sherry, if desired. Ladle into small bowls or mugs and top with
sour half-and-half or yogurt and a dash of paprika. Makes about 8
servings. Contains about 40 calories per serving.

French Tomato Soup

Chives and yogurt adorn this bright-red soup.

1 large onion, chopped
2 teaspoons butter
1 can (6 ounces) tomato paste
1 quart chicken stock
1 large tomato, peeled
salt and white pepper to taste
⅛ teaspoon freshly ground nutmeg
2 tablespoons low-fat yogurt
chopped chives or green onion tops for garnish

Using a large saucepot, sauté onion in butter until glazed and barely golden. Purée in the blender with tomato paste, 1 cup chicken stock, and tomato. Return to the saucepan with remaining chicken stock. Cover and simmer 15 minutes. Season with salt and pepper to taste and nutmeg. Serve in bowls and garnish with yogurt and chives. Makes 6 servings. Contains 50 calories per serving.

Watercress Soup

Spicy watercress lends snap to this first-course soup.

1 medium-sized onion
1 teaspoon butter
1 potato, peeled and diced
2 cups chicken broth
½ teaspoon each salt and crumbled dried tarragon
1 tablespoon cornstarch blended with 1 tablespoon cold water
1 bunch watercress, stems removed
¼ cup low-fat yogurt
few drops lemon juice

Sauté onion in butter in a large saucepan, cooking until glazed. Add potato, broth, salt, and tarragon. Cover and simmer until tender. Blend in a paste of cornstarch and cook until thickened. Pour into a blender container and blend with watercress and yogurt, just until cress is finely minced. Reheat without boiling and add a few drops of lemon juice. Serves 4. Contains 40 calories per serving.

Stracciatella

This zestful broth from Rome is zig-zagged with herb-streaked egg threads.

1 quart rich chicken or beef stock
2 eggs
¼ cup freshly shredded Romano or Parmesan cheese
2 tablespoons minced parsley
5 basil leaves, chopped, or ½ teaspoon dried basil

Heat broth to boiling. Beat eggs with cheese, parsley, and basil. Pour egg mixture into the boiling broth and remove pan from heat; do not stir. Ladle into soup bowls. Makes 8 first-course servings. Contains about 45 calories per serving.

Leek and Celery Root Soup

This mélange of winter vegetables makes a bracing supper soup.

2½ quarts rich beef stock (homemade, preferably, or use beef-stock base, diluted)
1 small celery root, peeled and diced
3 small carrots, peeled and sliced
1 bunch leeks, thoroughly washed and chopped
1 stalk celery, chopped
½ cup chopped celery leaves
salt and pepper to taste
freshly grated Romano cheese

Bring stock to a boil in a large soup kettle and add celery root and carrots. Cover and simmer 10 minutes. Add leeks, celery, and celery leaves and simmer 10 minutes longer. Season with salt and pepper to taste. Ladle into soup bowls and pass Romano cheese to sprinkle over it. Makes 8 servings. Contains about 100 calories per serving allowing 1 tablespoon cheese per person.

Egg Flower Soup

Notice the egg threads in this delicate ginger-seasoned broth.

1 quart chicken broth
2 teaspoons soy sauce
½ teaspoon shaved ginger root
¼ cup slivered roast pork or veal
2 green onions, chopped
1 egg

Bring broth to a boil and stir in soy sauce, ginger, slivered meat, and onions. Whisk egg until frothy and pour into the broth, swirling with a fork, and remove from heat. Makes 6 servings. Contains about 35 calories per serving.

Jamaican Carrot Soup

For an intriguing pass-around soup, try this carrot one.

**3 cups chicken stock or broth
1 small onion, chopped
4 carrots, peeled and sliced
⅛ teaspoon nutmeg
1 clove garlic, minced
1 tablespoon peanut butter
1 teaspoon Worcestershire
dash liquid hot pepper seasoning
salt and pepper to taste
chopped parsley or diced red-skinned apple for garnish**

Place in a saucepan the chicken stock, onion, carrots, nutmeg, garlic, peanut butter, Worcestershire, and pepper seasoning. Cover and simmer until vegetables are very tender, about 15 to 20 minutes. Cool slightly. Purée in a blender. Season with salt and pepper to taste. Ladle into small soup bowls or mugs and garnish with parsley. Makes 8 ½-cup first-course servings, or 4 to 6 luncheon-size servings. Contains about 25 calories per ½-cup serving.

Moroccan Meatball Soup

Fresh chopped cilantro and juicy tomatoes enliven this spicy full-meal soup. It's a marvelous meal by itself, with just a basket of apples to linger over at the end.

1 onion, chopped
1 carrot, peeled and grated
1 stalk celery, chopped
1 teaspoon oil
1½ quarts rich homemade beef stock or 1½ quarts water and 8 bouillon cubes
1 teaspoon grated fresh ginger root
½ teaspoon each cumin and seasoned pepper
salt to taste
3 tablespoons tomato paste
meatballs: see below
2 tomatoes, peeled and chopped
¼ cup chopped cilantro

Using a large soup kettle, sauté onion, carrot, and celery in oil until glazed. Add stock, ginger, cumin, pepper, salt, and tomato paste. Cover and simmer 25 minutes. Drop in meatballs and cook 15 minutes longer. If possible, cool and chill, then skim off any extra fat. Reheat and add chopped tomatoes and cilantro just before serving. Makes 6 servings. Contains 175 calories per serving.

Meatballs: Mix together 1 pound lean ground beef or lamb, 3 tablespoons cornstarch, 2 egg whites, 3 tablespoons minced cilantro, 1 clove chopped garlic, and 1 teaspoon salt. Shape into ¾-inch balls.

Early California Soup

The frontiersman Kit Carson is credited with creating this colorful chicken and vegetable soup. Its heritage stems from Mexico.

3-pound broiler-fryer
1 onion, peeled
4 whole cloves
1 stalk celery, cut up
2 teaspoons salt
6 whole peppercorns
½ teaspoon Mexican seasoning
1 ear corn, husked and cut in 1-inch slices
2 yellow crookneck squash, sliced
¼ cup chopped cilantro
2 tablespoons salted sunflower seeds
1 small avocado, peeled and diced
1 small red pepper, seeded and diced

Wash chicken and place in a soup kettle. Add 1½ quarts water, the onion stuck with cloves, celery, salt, and peppercorns. Cover and simmer 1 hour. Lift chicken from broth and cool. Remove meat from bones and cut into strips. Skim fat from broth, strain, and cook down until reduced to 5 cups. Bring to a boil and add Mexican seasoning, corn, and squash. Simmer 2 minutes. Add chicken and heat through. Ladle into bowls and sprinkle with cilantro and sunflower seeds. Sprinkle with avocado and red pepper. Serves 6. Contains about 200 calories per serving.

Chicken and Vegetable Soup

This combination of herbs and half a dozen vegetables — both roots and greens — makes an aromatic brew. Serve the chicken on the side if you like, or dice it into the soup.

6 cups freshly prepared chicken stock: see below
2 carrots, peeled and sliced
2 leeks (white part only), sliced
2 parsnips, peeled and sliced
2 turnips, peeled and diced
2 tablespoons cornstarch blended with 2 tablespoons cold water
1 bunch fresh spinach (leaves only)
1 head butter lettuce, cut into chunks
salt and freshly ground pepper to taste
sour half-and-half
chopped parsley

Bring chicken stock to a boil and add carrots, leeks, parsnips, and turnips. Cover and simmer about 20 minutes, or until vegetables are tender. Bring to a boil and stir in a paste of cornstarch and water. Cook until thickened. Add spinach and lettuce and heat through. Season with salt and pepper. Ladle into bowls and garnish with sour half-and-half and parsley. Serves 8. Contains about 40 calories per serving.

Chicken Stock: Place in a large kettle a 3-pound broiler-fryer, 1½ quarts water, 2 teaspoons salt, 1 quartered onion, 1 stalk celery, and 1 peeled, halved carrot. Cover and simmer 1 hour. Remove chicken, strain stock, and skim fat.

Fish Ball Soup

Cilantro and ginger spice the plump fish balls in this fragrant Oriental soup.

2 quarts rich fish stock: see below
1 pound turbot fillets
8 water chestnuts
2 ounces small cooked shrimp
2 slices fresh ginger root, chopped
2 green onions, chopped
1 teaspoon salt
1 tablespoon dry Sherry
¼ cup water
2 egg whites
1 teaspoon cornstarch
1 carrot, peeled and sliced
3 tablespoons minced cilantro

First prepare fish stock. Then put the fish fillets and water chestnuts through a food chopper. Mix in shrimp, ginger, 1 onion, salt, Sherry, water, egg whites, and cornstarch, and beat until mixture adheres in a fluffy consistency. Bring stock to a boil. Shape fish mixture into 1-inch balls and drop into the stock. Add carrots and cook until fish balls are cooked through, about 10 minutes. Add remaining green onion and cilantro. Ladle into bowls. Serves 4 to 6. Contains 100 to 150 calories per serving.

Fish Stock: Simmer fish heads and bones with onion, celery, and *bouquet garni* for 30 minutes. Strain. (Or use equal parts clam juice and water.)

Seafood Soup, Italian Style

Try this invigorating fish stew for a party supper with a green salad and fruit platter.

1 large onion, chopped
1 carrot, peeled and chopped
1 stalk celery, chopped
1 clove garlic, minced
1 teaspoon salad or olive oil
1 can (8 ounces) tomato sauce
1 can (8 ounces) minced clams
1 cup fish stock or clam juice
½ cup each water and dry white wine
2 tablespoons white-wine vinegar
½ teaspoon crumbled dried orégano
salt and pepper
1 pound turbot fillets or other boneless white fish
2 tomatoes, peeled and chopped
¼ cup chopped parsley

Using a large saucepan or soup pot, sauté onion, carrot, celery, and garlic in oil until limp. Add tomato sauce, clams and their juice, fish stock, water, wine, vinegar, orégano, and salt and pepper to taste. Cover and simmer 10 minutes. Add turbot and tomatoes and simmer 10 minutes longer. Use a fork to break the fish into bite-sized pieces. Sprinkle with parsley. Makes 4 servings. Contains about 190 calories per serving.

Salads

As the seasons turn, the greengrocer's produce composes the table fare. The local bounty shows off to advantage in salads. Not only do fruits and vegetables reflect the nature of the season, herbs do likewise. Remember to pluck a wisp of fresh dill for Swedish-Style Cucumbers, adorn an Italian salad with pungent petals of basil, and strew cilantro over Tossed Shredded Chicken Salad.

You may use a blender to make up the French Shallot Dressing in quantity and store it in a capped slender-necked bottle in the refrigerator. It makes a good "House Dressing" as it is so versatile. It is perfect for any green salad, or cold cooked vegetables. The marketplace and the refrigerator may dictate what embellishments go into the bowl along with the greens. The potpourri of choices includes sliced red peppers, cantaloupe spears, alfalfa sprouts, sunflower seeds, chunks of feta, diagonally-cut asparagus, wafer-thin zucchini, spears of winter pears, green grapes, shredded red or Chinese cabbage, and diced red-skinned apples and avocado.

French Shallot Salad

A zestful shallot and mustard dressing coats tender butter lettuce or any green salad. Try it on cold, cooked artichoke hearts, asparagus, green beans, or raw sliced mushrooms.

1 large head butter lettuce, washed and chilled (or romaine, or a combination of greens)
3 tablespoons safflower oil
1½ tablespoons red-wine vinegar
⅛ teaspoon salt
½ teaspoon Dijon-style mustard
1 shallot, finely chopped
freshly ground pepper

Tear greens into bite-sized pieces. Place in a salad bowl the oil, vinegar, salt, mustard, and shallot and stir to blend. Add greens and mix until coated. Grind pepper over all. Makes 4 servings. Contains about 85 calories per serving.

Asparagus Vinaigrette Salad

A light lemon dressing sharpens this cold salad plate of fresh cooked asparagus and avocado crescents.

1½ pounds fresh asparagus spears
greens
1 avocado
1 tablespoon each lemon juice and white-wine vinegar
3 tablespoons salad or olive oil
½ teaspoon each salt and Dijon-style mustard
1 teaspoon minced shallots
2 teaspoons chopped capers
2 strips crumbled cooked bacon

Cook asparagus in boiling salted water until crisp tender; cool and chill. Arrange greens on a serving platter and top with bundles of asparagus. Peel and slice avocado very thinly and arrange on top. Mix together the lemon juice, vinegar, oil, salt, mustard, shallots, and capers. Spoon over salad and sprinkle with bacon. Makes 6 servings. Contains about 150 calories per serving.

Caesar-Style Salad

A creamy egg and Parmesan cheese dressing enhances the crisp
bite of romaine.

1 head romaine, washed and crisped
1 egg
2 tablespoons olive oil
1 tablespoon each lemon juice and white-wine vinegar
½ teaspoon each Dijon-style mustard and anchovy paste
⅛ teaspoon salt
pepper to taste
¼ cup freshly shredded Parmesan cheese

Break salad greens into bite-sized pieces. Beat together with a wire
whisk just until blended the egg, oil, lemon juice, vinegar, mustard,
anchovy paste, and salt. Pour over greens and mix lightly. Grind over
pepper and sprinkle with cheese. Makes 4 servings. Contains about
100 calories per serving.

Tri-Color Salad

Tomatoes, mozzarella, and pungent fresh basil leaves reflect the red,
white, and green colors of the Italian flag in this seasonal
summer salad.

3 large tomatoes
1 tablespoon olive oil
salt and pepper to taste
2 ounces mozzarella cheese, thinly sliced
12 fresh basil leaves

Peel and slice tomatoes and arrange on a platter. Drizzle with oil and
sprinkle with salt and pepper. Overlap cheese slices on tomatoes and
cluster basil in the center. Makes 4 servings. Contains about 90
calories per serving.

Spinach and Egg Salad with Thousand Island Dressing

Fresh spinach has a healthy impact when you taste this salad garnished with shredded egg.

1 large bunch spinach, washed and torn into bits
3 tablespoons each sour half-and-half and yogurt
2 tablespoons chili sauce
2 teaspoons lemon juice
dash each Worcestershire and Tabasco
salt and pepper to taste
1 hard-cooked egg, shredded
1 tablespoon chopped chives or green onions

Mound spinach on individual salad plates. Mix together the sour half-and-half, yogurt, chili sauce, lemon juice, Worcestershire, Tabasco, salt, and pepper. Spoon over the spinach. Shred the egg on top and sprinkle with chives. Makes 4 servings. Contains about 60 calories per serving.

Spinach and Bacon Salad

A tasteful blend of spices punctuates the dressing for this cool spinach salad.

2 tablespoons white-wine vinegar
1 tablespoon dry white wine
1 teaspoon soy sauce
½ teaspoon each salt, sugar, dry mustard, and curry powder
¼ teaspoon ground black pepper
¼ cup safflower oil
1 large bunch spinach, washed and chilled
4 slices crumbled cooked bacon
1 hard-cooked egg

Combine the vinegar, wine, soy sauce, salt, sugar, mustard, curry powder, and pepper, stirring until dissolved. Mix in the oil. Shake well and chill. Tear spinach into bite-sized pieces and place in a salad bowl. Pour over dressing, mix thoroughly, and sprinkle with bacon and sieved egg. Makes 4 servings. Contains 150 calories per serving.

Note: Instead of spinach, substitute the inner head of romaine for a pleasing combination.

Green Salad with Cucumber Dressing

This cucumber buttermilk dressing is equally tempting spooned over sliced oranges.

⅓ cup buttermilk
2 tablespoons cottage cheese
1½ tablespoons lemon juice
½ teaspoon each salt and dill weed
freshly ground pepper
½ cucumber, peeled and diced
⅓ cup diced red pepper or sliced radishes
4 cups torn iceberg lettuce

Blend together the buttermilk, cottage cheese, lemon juice, salt, dill weed, and pepper. Mix in cucumber and red pepper. Toss with greens. Makes 4 servings. Contains about 35 calories per serving.

Papaya and Crab Salad

Tropical papaya half shells provide an exotic container for a seafood salad.

2 papayas
greens
1 pound Dungeness or king crab meat or small cooked shrimp or lobster
cherry tomatoes
⅓ cup each sour half-and-half and yogurt
2 tablespoons each chili sauce and lime juice
2 tablespoons chopped chives
dash salt and pepper

Peel, halve, and scoop out seeds of the papaya. Arrange on greens and fill the center shells with seafood. Garnish with cherry tomatoes. For dressing, blend together the half-and-half, yogurt, chili sauce, lime juice, chives, salt, and pepper. Pass to spoon over salad. Makes 4 servings. Contains about 175 calories per serving.

Swedish-Style Cucumbers

Pickled cucumbers provide a sprightly relish-salad to complement fish and seafood.

2 large cucumbers
¼ cup tarragon-flavored white-wine vinegar
1 tablespoon water
2 tablespoons sugar
¼ teaspoon salt
freshly ground pepper
1 teaspoon chopped fresh dill (optional)
2 tablespoons chopped parsley

Leave the peel on half of a cucumber and peel remaining cucumbers; slice thinly and place in a deep bowl. Mix together vinegar, water, sugar, salt, pepper, dill, and parsley and pour over cucumbers. Mix well, cover, and chill at least 4 hours, stirring once or twice. Makes 6 servings. Contains about 20 calories per serving.

Blue Cheese Dressing

Punctuated with cheese, this creamy dressing is excellent tossed with greens or spooned over sliced tomatoes or cooked and chilled vegetables such as green beans, asparagus spears, or artichoke hearts.

½ cup buttermilk
¼ cup cottage cheese
2 ounces blue cheese
4 teaspoons white-wine vinegar
½ teaspoon each garlic salt and Worcestershire
1 shallot, peeled, or 1 green onion, chopped

Place in a blender container the buttermilk, cottage cheese, blue cheese, vinegar, garlic salt, Worcestershire, and shallot. Blend until smooth. Pour into a jar, cover, and chill. Makes 1 cup. Contains about 16 calories per tablespoon.

Salad Horiatika

This Greek country salad is a meal by itself — perfect for a summer lunch.

4 large tomatoes
2 medium-sized cucumbers
1 small sweet onion
½ head iceberg lettuce or endive or chicory
1 dozen Mediterranean-style olives
¼ cup olive oil
2 tablespoons red-wine vinegar
¼ teaspoon salt
½ teaspoon crumbled dried orégano
freshly ground pepper
4 ounces feta cheese
1 tablespoon big capers

Core tomatoes and cut into wedges. Peel and halve the cucumber lengthwise, then slice. Peel and slice the onion thinly. Tear lettuce into bite-sized pieces. Place them in a salad bowl along with the olives. Mix together the oil, vinegar, salt, orégano, and pepper. Pour over the salad and toss. Dice or crumble the cheese and scatter cheese and capers over the salad. Makes 4 servings. Contains 275 calories per serving.

Fennel and Blue Cheese Salad

Anise-flavored fennel, radishes, and blue cheese are stimulating companions in this colorful first-course or luncheon salad.

2 large fennel bulbs
6 radishes
1 small cucumber
⅓ cup safflower or olive oil
1½ tablespoons each white-wine vinegar and lemon juice
1 teaspoon Dijon-style mustard
½ teaspoon salt
freshly ground pepper
1 green onion or shallot, chopped
2 tablespoons chopped parsley
endive or chicory
2 ounces crumbled blue cheese
3 hard-cooked eggs, cut in wedges
1 dozen cherry tomatoes, halved
Mediterranean olives (optional)

Trim fennel and slice thinly. Place in a salad bowl. Slice radishes and add to bowl. Peel and halve cucumber lengthwise, then slice and add to bowl. Combine the oil, vinegar, lemon juice, mustard, salt, and pepper; whisk until blended. Mix in onion and parsley, and pour over the salad. Mix well. Spoon onto endive arranged on a flat platter and scatter cheese over it. Ring with eggs, tomatoes, and olives. Serves 6. Contains 175 calories per serving.

Pepper, Pear, and Cheese Plate

For an easy fall lunch, consider this striking salad medley. It offers a captivating range of flavors.

1 bunch watercress
2 large Bartlett pears
1 sweet red bell pepper
2 ounces blue cheese
1 teaspoon sunflower seeds

Arrange sprigs of watercress on two luncheon plates. Slice pears lengthwise, discarding core, and arrange slices on each plate. Halve pepper, remove seeds, and cut into thin strips. Scatter over the pears. Crumble the cheese over the salad and sprinkle it with seeds. Makes 2 servings. Contains about 195 calories per serving.

Egg and Anchovy Salad

A simple butter lettuce salad is enlivened by anchovy and the tender bite of shredded egg.

3 tablespoons safflower oil
1½ tablespoons red- or white-wine vinegar
1 teaspoon Dijon-style mustard
1 teaspoon chopped shallots
¼ teaspoon salt
1 head butter lettuce (about 1 quart torn greens)
1 hard-cooked egg, shredded
3 anchovies, minced

For dressing, mix together oil, vinegar, mustard, shallots, and salt. Place greens in a bowl, pour on dressing, and mix lightly. Scatter the egg and anchovies over it and mix again. Makes 4 generous servings. Contains 100 calories per serving.

Turkish Salad Tray

Barbecued shish kebab goes well with this colorful composed salad.

1 cucumber, thinly sliced
1 bunch radishes, thinly sliced
1 red pepper, seeded and diced
1 green pepper, seeded and diced
3 tomatoes, peeled and cut in wedges
½ bunch chicory or endive, thinly sliced
1 bunch green onions, chopped
2 ounces diced feta cheese
orégano dressing: see below

Arrange on a tray in separate sections the cucumber, radishes, peppers, tomatoes, chicory, and onions. Place feta in a small bowl alongside. At serving time, drizzle salad with Orégano Dressing and serve on individual plates. Scatter the cheese over it. Makes 6 servings. Contains about 120 calories per serving.

Orégano Dressing: Mix together 2 tablespoons red-wine vinegar, 1 tablespoon lemon juice, ¼ cup olive oil, 2 tablespoons minced parsley, ¾ teaspoon dried orégano, teaspoon salt, and freshly ground pepper to taste.

Cantaloupe Shrimp Boats

Small cantaloupes cut in half zig-zag fashion form bowls for a seafood salad.

2 small cantaloupes
romaine leaves
1 cup diced celery
1 pound small cooked shrimp
green goddess yogurt dressing: see below

With a sharp-pointed knife, cut cantaloupes in half by making zig-zag cuts. Scoop out seeds. Use a serrated knife to remove the flesh from the shell, then chop it into bite-sized pieces. Line each shell with romaine leaves. Mix together the diced fruit, celery, and shrimp, and pile into the melon shells. Cover and chill until serving time. Serve on a salad plate and pass a pitcher of dressing. Makes 4 servings. Contains about 175 calories per serving.

Green Goddess Yogurt Dressing: Stir together 2 tablespoons white-wine vinegar, 1 teaspoon dried tarragon, 1 chopped green onion, 2 tablespoons minced parsley, 2 teaspoons anchovy paste, 1 teaspoon sugar, ½ teaspoon salt, and 1 cup low-fat yogurt. Makes about 1¼ cups (about 9 calories per tablespoon).

Mexican Tray Salad

This handsome fruit and vegetable platter is a natural accompaniment for spicy Mexican meats or fish.

1 large cucumber, scored and sliced
3 tablespoons white-wine vinegar
1 tablespoon olive oil
½ teaspoon salt
butter lettuce
3 navel oranges, peeled and thinly sliced
1 sweet red onion, peeled and sliced
1 large avocado, peeled and sliced
2 teaspoons lemon juice
spicy orange dressing: see below

Place cucumber in a bowl and mix with vinegar, oil, and salt; let stand 1 hour. Line a large tray with greens and arrange on it in separate sections the sliced cucumber (use slotted spoon), sliced oranges, onion, and avocado, drizzled with lemon juice. Spoon over it Spicy Orange Dressing. Makes 6 servings. Contains about 110 calories per serving.

Spicy Orange Dressing: Mix together ¼ cup orange juice, 1 teaspoon grated lemon peel, 1 teaspoon Mexican seasoning, and dash salt.

Salad Niçoise

A lattice of anchovies and olives looks festive on this French country salad.

1 head butter lettuce
1 can (6 or 7 ounces) white albacore tuna
1 package (10 ounces) Italian green beans, parboiled and chilled
1 English cucumber
1 can (2 ounces) anchovy fillets
milk
1 dozen large black pitted olives
½ pound cherry tomatoes
3 hard-cooked eggs, quartered
2 tablespoons olive oil
1½ tablespoons white-wine vinegar
salt and freshly ground black pepper
1 teaspoon each Dijon-style mustard and chopped shallots
1 tablespoon chopped parsley

Arrange washed, crisped leaves of butter lettuce on a shallow platter. Flake tuna and scatter over lettuce. Sprinkle with beans. Thinly slice cucumber, with peel on, and arrange on top, overlapping the slices. Soak anchovies in milk a few minutes to reduce the strong flavor, then cut them into thin strips. Arrange in a lattice over the cucumber. Halve olives lengthwise and place in each square. Halve cherry tomatoes and alternate them with the egg quarters around the dish. Mix the oil, vinegar, salt, pepper, mustard, shallots, and parsley and pour over the salad. Makes 4 servings. Contains 170 calories per serving.

Tossed Shredded Chicken Salad

Fresh cilantro is a must for this Oriental full-meal salad, as it lends the authentic spiciness that is so appealing.

1 pound chicken breasts
½ cup chicken broth
1 medium-sized head iceberg lettuce, shredded
4 green onions, thinly sliced
1 small bunch cilantro
1 can (4 ounces) water chestnuts, very thinly sliced
1 stalk celery, very thinly sliced
½ cup cooked petit peas (optional)
3 radishes, very thinly sliced
¼ cup toasted sesame seeds
1 avocado, sliced, or 4 slices or spears fresh pineapple
sesame oil dressing: see below

Poach chicken breasts in broth for 15 minutes, or until cooked through. Let cool, then remove skin and bones and dice meat finely. (Use broth for another recipe.) Place chicken in a bowl with lettuce, onions, cilantro sprigs, water chestnuts, celery, peas (if desired), and radishes. Pour Sesame Oil Dressing over salad and mix well. Spoon into serving bowls and sprinkle with sesame seeds. Garnish with avocado slices or fresh pineapple. Makes 4 servings. Contains about 310 calories per serving.

Sesame Oil Dressing: Mix together in a small container 1 teaspoon salt, dash Tabasco, ½ teaspoon each dry mustard and grated lemon peel, 1½ teaspoons white-wine vinegar, 1 tablespoon each honey and soy sauce, and 2 tablespoons each sesame oil, lemon juice, and safflower oil.

Fish and Seafood

Poached, baked, and broiled fish and swiftly stir-fried seafood offer some of the most rewarding entrées. Remarkably low in calories, they are also one of the best sources of protein. Naturally, quality depends on freshness and precise timing.

This selection is drawn from a wealth of favorites sampled abroad. In Avignon at Hiely's two-star restaurant, Clam and Spinach Shells are set forth piping hot in individual copper ramekins. Sailing from Stockholm to Helsinki, the midnight *smörgåsboard* spread displays a dozen crocks of pickled fish, some with onion rings as in our recipe. Lobster Tails with Macadamia Butter are a Hawaiian delicacy, and Sole Veronique reminds me of an Alsatian one-star restaurant nestled in the woods.

While certain fish are specified in each recipe, others can certainly replace them. Sole, turbot, and red snapper are interchangeable, as are swordfish, halibut, and *mahi mahi*.

Scallops Almondine

Succulent, wine-poached scallops make a rich-tasting entrée with a surprisingly low calorie count.

2 tablespoons chicken or clam broth
¼ teaspoon salt
1 pound scallops, cut in half
2 tablespoons dry Vermouth or dry white wine
½ teaspoon crumbled dried tarragon
2 tablespoons sliced, unblanched almonds, oven-toasted

Heat broth and salt in a large frying pan. Add scallops, cover, bring to a boil, and simmer 5 minutes, or until scallops lose their transparency. Add Vermouth and tarragon and simmer 1 minute longer. Sprinkle with almonds. Makes 4 servings. Contains about 125 calories per serving.

Crab-Stuffed Artichokes

Fresh seafood stuffed inside plump, cold cooked artichokes makes a
wonderful supper entrée or party luncheon salad.

2 tablespoons minced parsley
1 shallot or green onion, chopped
1½ tablespoons lemon juice
2 teaspoons olive oil
½ teaspoon salt
dash liquid hot pepper seasoning
¼ teaspoon crumbled dried tarragon
1 pound Dungeness crab, small cooked shrimp, or lobster
4 large, whole cooked artichokes
greens
green goddess yogurt dressing: see page 67

Mix together in a bowl the parsley, shallot, lemon juice, oil, salt, hot
pepper seasoning, and tarragon. Add seafood and mix lightly. Cover
and chill. Trim off stem end of each artichoke and scoop out center
choke. Gently spread open leaves slightly and spoon marinated seafood
into the center of each. Arrange on greens and pass Green Goddess
Yogurt Dressing. Serves 4. Contains about 175 calories per salad, plus
9 calories per tablespoon of dressing.

Shrimp and Crab Chantilly

A soufflé-like topping masks the seafood in this ultra low-calorie entrée.

2 teaspoons whipped margarine
1 tablespoon chopped shallots or green onions
½ pound each crab meat and small cooked shrimp
3 tablespoons dry white wine
½ teaspoon each salt and crumbled dried tarragon
4 egg whites
1 tablespoon cornstarch
2 teaspoons Dijon-style mustard
½ teaspoon salt
dash Tabasco
2 tablespoons grated Romano or Parmesan cheese

Melt margarine in a large frying pan and sauté the shallots. Add crab and shrimp and stir until heated. Add wine, salt, and tarragon and cook down until evaporated. Spread in a lightly greased 1½-quart baking dish. Beat egg whites until soft peaks form. Add the cornstarch, beating until stiff. Stir in mustard, salt, and Tabasco. Spread over seafood and sprinkle with cheese. Bake in a 375° oven for 20 minutes or until lightly browned. Makes 4 servings. Contains about 135 calories per serving.

Clam and Spinach Shells

Scallop shells make charming containers for this seafood course.

2 green onions or shallots, chopped
1 teaspoon butter
1 can (7½ ounces) minced clams
3 tablespoons dry white wine
3 tablespoons nonfat dry milk solids dissolved in ¼ cup water
1 tablespoon cornstarch blended with 1 tablespoon cold water
¼ teaspoon each salt and tarragon
1 bunch spinach, finely chopped, or 1 package (10 ounces) frozen
chopped spinach, thawed and squeezed dry
1 tablespoon each shredded Parmesan and Gruyère cheese

Sauté onions in butter in a large frying pan. Add clams and liquid, wine, milk, and cornstarch paste. Bring to a boil and, stirring, cook until thickened. Add salt, tarragon, and spinach and cook until spinach is heated through. Spoon into buttered scallop shells and sprinkle with cheese. Bake in a 400° oven until the top is golden brown, about 10 minutes. Serves 3. Contains about 75 calories per serving.

Note: For a more substantial dish, nestle a poached egg in each spinach bed, sprinkle with cheese, and oven bake 5 to 10 minutes.

Shrimp and Mushroom Crêpes

Feathery light crêpes, based on cornstarch for thickening, encase a
seafood filling.

crêpes: see below
½ pound turbot or sole fillets
½ cup water
¼ cup dry Vermouth
½ teaspoon each salt and tarragon
¼ cup nonfat dry milk solids
3 tablespoons cornstarch blended with 3 tablespoons cold water
½ pound mushrooms, sliced
2 shallots, chopped
1½ teaspoons butter
¾ pound small cooked shrimp
½ teaspoon grated lemon peel
¼ cup shredded Romano or Parmesan cheese

First prepare crêpes as below. Poach turbot in water, Vermouth, salt,
and tarragon for 5 minutes, or until it flakes with a fork; remove fish
from pan. Bring stock to a boil and stir in milk solids. Combine
cornstarch and water and add to pan. Cook, stirring, until thickened.
Sauté mushrooms and shallots in butter just until glazed. Add
shrimp and lemon peel and cook 1 minute. Mix in flaked fish, sauce,
and half the cheese. Place a spoonful on each crêpe and roll up. Place in
a greased baking dish and repeat until all the crêpes are filled. Sprinkle
with remaining cheese. Bake in a 375° oven for 10 minutes. Makes 6
servings, allowing 2 crêpes apiece. Contains 75 calories per serving.

Crêpes: Place in a blender container 3 eggs, ¼ cup each nonfat dry
milk solids and cornstarch, ¾ cup water, and ½ teaspoon salt. Blend
just until smooth. Pour about 3 tablespoons batter into a lightly
buttered hot crêpe pan and cook until browned underneath. Remove
from pan and repeat with remaining batter. Makes about 12 crepes, 6
to 7 inches in diameter.

Shrimp and Snow Peas

Glistening green edible pea pods and pretty pink shrimp offer an eye-catching entrée. (By the way, pea pods are unbelievably low in calorie count — just 1 calorie per pod.)

6 ounces edible pod peas
¾ pound medium-sized raw shrimp
1 tablespoon peanut or safflower oil
½ teaspoon salt
⅓ cup clam juice or chicken stock
1 small onion, cut in half, then into small wedges
1 small stalk celery, cut diagonally
½ teaspoon monosodium glutamate (optional)
1 teaspoon soy sauce
1½ teaspoons cornstarch dissolved in 1 tablespoon cold water

Break off stem ends of pea pods and pull off strings. Peel and butterfly shrimp and wash out the sand vein. Heat a wok or large frying pan, add oil, salt, and shrimp and stir and cook for 1 minute or until shrimp turn pink. Add clam juice or stock, peas, onion, and celery. Cover and cook 2 minutes, stirring once or twice. Add monosodium glutamate, soy sauce, and cornstarch mixture and cook, stirring, until thickened. Serves 4, but do include another vegetable-entrée dish. Contains about 110 calories per serving.

Asparagus and Eggs Scandinavian

Tiny flambéed shrimp enhance a simple asparagus and poached egg
dish.

1 pound asparagus spears, cut about 4 inches long
4 poached eggs
1 tablespoon butter or margarine
¼ teaspoon crumbled dried tarragon
½ pound small cooked shrimp
1 tablespoon brandy or Cognac
salt and pepper to taste
1 tablespoon each finely shredded Gruyère and chopped parsley

Cook asparagus in boiling salted water or a steamer until crisp tender,
about 5 to 7 minutes; drain. Arrange in a greased baking dish and
nestle poached eggs on top. Melt butter in a frying pan, add tarragon
and shrimp, and heat through. Warm brandy, ignite, and pour over
shrimp, shaking pan. When flame burns out, spoon shrimp and juices
over asparagus and eggs. Sprinkle with salt and pepper to taste.
Sprinkle with cheese and parsley. Makes 4 servings. Contains about
170 calories per serving.

Lobster Tails or Sole with Macadamia Butter

Butter-browned macadamia nuts lend elegance to broiled shellfish.

4 lobster tails (about 6 ounces each)
1 tablespoon melted butter or margarine
¼ cup chopped macadamia nuts
lemon wedges
watercress or parsley sprigs for garnish

Split lobster tails in half lengthwise. Drop into boiling salted water and simmer gently for 6 minutes, or until no longer translucent. Drain. Arrange tails on a baking sheet and brush with 1½ teaspoons butter. Place under the broiler and broil until just lightly browned, about 4 to 5 minutes. Heat remaining butter until it starts to brown; add nuts and heat slightly. Spoon over lobster and garnish with lemon wedges and watercress. Makes 4 servings. Contains about 200 calories per serving.

Note: You may substitute 1 pound sole or turbot fillets for the lobster. Arrange fish on a foil-lined pan, brush with butter, and season lightly with salt, seasoned pepper, and paprika. Broil about 4 minutes, or until lightly browned, broiling one side only.

Sole Veronique

Plump green grapes make a tart finish on this quickly broiled fish entrée.

1 cup Ladyfinger or Muscat grapes, halved and seeded
2 tablespoons dry white wine
1 pound sole or turbot fillets
1 tablespoon lemon juice
salt and pepper to taste
½ teaspoon salad supreme seasoning or seasoning salt
½ teaspoon grated orange peel
1 teaspoon butter or margarine
1 orange, cut in slices
watercress sprigs

Place grapes in a bowl and sprinkle with wine. Arrange fish fillets on a sheet of foil on a broiling pan and drizzle with lemon juice. Season with salt, pepper, salad supreme seasoning, and orange peel. Dot with butter. Broil until golden brown, about 5 minutes. Arrange grapes over the top, cut side down, and broil about 30 seconds longer. Garnish each serving with an orange slice and a small bunch of watercress. Makes 4 servings. Contains about 150 calories per serving.

Soufflé-Topped Sole

A golden soufflé caps sole for an impressive entrée to bring to the table.

1 pound sole or turbot fillets
½ cup fish stock or clam juice
1 tablespoon lemon juice
1½ teaspoons each salt and dried tarragon
¼ cup nonfat dry milk powder
2 tablespoons each cornstarch and water
2 eggs, separated
3 egg whites
¼ cup grated Parmesan or Romano cheese

Place fish, fish stock, lemon juice, salt, and tarragon in a frying pan. Cover and simmer for 5 minutes, or until fish is barely cooked through. Lift out to a 10-inch round shallow baking dish. Cook down liquid until reduced to ¾ cup. Blend in dry milk powder and bring to a boil. Stir in a paste of cornstarch and water and cook until thickened. Mix in egg yolks and half the cheese. Beat the 5 egg whites until stiff but not dry and fold into sauce. Spread over fish and sprinkle with remaining cheese. Bake in a 400° oven for 20 to 25 minutes or until puffed and golden brown. Makes 4 servings. Contains 225 calories per serving.

Turbot in a Parsley Cloak

Green parsley and crimson cherry tomatoes make a brilliant splash on turbot.

1 pound turbot or sole fillets
salt, pepper, and garlic salt to taste
⅓ cup finely chopped parsley
2 green onions, chopped
½ teaspoon crumbled dried basil
1 teaspoon grated orange or lemon peel
2 teaspoons safflower or corn oil
1 dozen cherry tomatoes, halved

Arrange fish in a lightly buttered baking dish and season with salt, pepper, and garlic salt. Mix together the parsley, onions, basil, citrus peel, and oil and strew over fish. Arrange tomatoes cut side down on top. Bake uncovered in a 375° oven for 20 minutes or until fish flakes with a fork. Makes 4 servings. Contains about 140 calories per serving.

Turbot in a Yogurt Mask

A golden herb-flavored topping masks fish fillets.

1 pound turbot or sole fillets
salt and pepper to taste
½ cup low-fat yogurt
2 tablespoons dry white wine
1 egg yolk
1 green onion, chopped
⅛ teaspoon garlic salt
3 tablespoons minced parsley

Lay fish fillets in a lightly greased baking dish and sprinkle with salt and pepper. Stir together the yogurt, wine, egg yolk, onion, garlic salt, and parsley and spread over the fish, covering completely. Bake in a 375° oven for 20 minutes or until fish flakes with a fork. Serves 4. Contains 150 calories per serving.

Fish Fillets Mexicali

A mélange of fresh chopped vegetables and spices blankets fish fillets for a striking entrée.

1 pound turbot or sole fillets (about 4 fillets)
1 teaspoon Mexican seasoning (combination of orégano, cumin, garlic, and chile peppers)
2 green onions, chopped
½ red or green pepper, seeds removed and chopped
2 tomatoes, peeled and chopped
2 tablespoons each chopped parsley and cilantro
½ teaspoon garlic salt
1 teaspoon shredded fresh ginger root
1 small avocado
lemon wedges

Arrange fish fillets in a lightly buttered baking dish and sprinkle with half the Mexican seasoning. Mix together green onions, peppers, tomatoes, parsley, cilantro, garlic salt, ginger root, and remaining Mexican seasoning and spoon over the fish. Bake in a 375° oven for 20 minutes or until fish flakes with a fork. Peel and slice avocado and arrange 2 slices on each serving. Garnish with lemon wedges. Makes 4 servings. Contains about 190 calories per serving.

Skewered Swordfish

To compose this colorful kebab entrée, alternate swordfish with cherry tomatoes and feathers of bay.

3 tablespoons dry Vermouth
1½ tablespoons lemon juice
1 tablespoon olive oil
½ teaspoon each salt and dried orégano
1 clove garlic, minced
1 green onion, chopped
1 pound swordfish or halibut steaks, cut about ¾-inch thick
1 dozen cherry tomatoes
1 dozen fresh bay leaves (optional)
1 lemon, cut in wedges

Mix together in a bowl the Vermouth, lemon juice, oil, salt, orégano, garlic, and onion. Cut fish into 1¼-inch squares, place in the marinade, cover, and chill several hours, turning. Alternate on skewers the fish, tomatoes, and bay leaves (use freshly picked ones or omit as dry ones will burn). Place on a broiler pan and broil about 10 minutes, turning, basting with marinade. Accompany with lemon wedges. Serves 4.
Contains about 170 calories per serving.

Pickled Fish and Onion Rings

Spiced pickled fish, spooned from a crock, offers a tantalizing summer picnic entrée. Serve on Swedish-style rye krisp or rye wafers and accompany with fresh cucumbers and cherry tomatoes.

2 pounds boneless fish steaks or fillets, such as halibut or turbot
3 slices lemon
1 teaspoon salt
1 teaspoon mixed pickling spice, tied in a cheesecloth bag
1 bay leaf
1 sweet red onion, sliced and separated into rings
⅔ cup tarragon-flavored white-wine vinegar
½ cup dry Vermouth or dry white wine
6 each whole allspice and peppercorns
3 tablespoons sugar

Place fish in a kettle, cover with water, and add lemon, salt, pickling spice, and bay leaf. Cover and bring to a boil and let simmer 5 to 10 minutes, or until fish flakes with a fork. Drain off liquid and let fish cool. Remove any bones or skin and separate fish along its natural seams into 1½-inch chunks. Alternate fish and onion rings in a 1½-quart jar or crock. Combine in a saucepan the vinegar, Vermouth or wine, allspice, peppercorns, and sugar. Bring to a boil and simmer until sugar dissolves. Pour over fish. Cover and chill several hours or up to 2 days. Makes 8 servings. Contains about 125 calories per serving.

Whaling Station Bouillabaisse

An assorted array of fish and shellfish, still with shells on, simmers into a succulent soup-stew.

1 onion, chopped
1 leek, chopped (white part only)
1 teaspoon olive oil
2 cloves garlic, minced
1 cup dry white wine
1 quart fish stock or water and part clam juice
few celery leaves
salt and pepper to taste
1 dozen raw rock clams in their shells
8 large raw shrimp
1½ pounds assorted fish: halibut, turbot fillets, red snapper, rock cod, sea bass

Using a large soup kettle, sauté onion and leek in oil until limp. Add garlic, wine, stock, celery leaves, and salt and pepper. Cover and simmer 15 minutes. Add clams, shrimp, and fish and simmer 10 to 15 minutes longer, or until fish is cooked through. Ladle into large bowls. Makes 4 generous servings. Contains about 250 calories per serving.

Poultry

Plump chickens roast to juicy succulence when left whole, as the thin layering of fat underneath the skin automatically self-bastes them. At serving time, you can neatly remove the fatty skin. The French method of seasoning a humble bird with fruit, herbs, or vegetables dominates this section.

A novel ingredient available in many supermarkets is ground turkey meat, a choice high-protein, low-fat product that hardly resembles turkey when spiced and seasoned. It stands in nicely for ground veal in a meat loaf, terrine, or meat balls.

Roast Chicken with Grapes

The grapes burst with juiciness after roasting in the bird.

3-pound broiler-fryer
1 tablespoon lemon juice
1 teaspoon grated lemon peel
salt, pepper, and paprika
1½ cups seedless grapes
⅓ cup dry white wine

Wash chicken and pat dry. Rub with lemon juice and sprinkle with salt, pepper, and paprika. Place on a roasting pan and stuff the cavity with the whole grapes. Roast in a 400° oven for 20 minutes; reduce heat to 325° and roast 1 to 1¼ hours longer, or until the drumstick moves easily, basting several times with wine and drippings. Carve and serve grapes alongside. Pass pan juices skimmed of fat. Makes 4 to 6 servings. Contains about 200 to 250 calories per serving.

Fruit Garland Roast Chicken

A della Robbia wreath of summertime fruits surrounds a golden roast chicken for a guest entrée.

4½- to 5-pound roasting chicken
lemon marinade: see below
1 small lemon, quartered
celery leaves
1 papaya
1 small avocado
1 cup strawberries with stems

Wash chicken and pat dry. Place in a large bowl, pour lemon-herb marinade over it, cover, and chill at least 2 hours, turning. Drain off marinade and reserve. Tuck quartered lemon and a few celery leaves inside chicken cavity. Place chicken on a rack in an uncovered pan and roast in a 350° oven about 2 hours or until the thickest part of the drumstick yields to gentle pressure. Baste several times with marinade. (Or impale the chicken on a spit and barbecue according to directions for your specific barbecue.)

For fruit garland, peel and slice papaya and avocado, discarding seeds. Wash strawberries. Place roasted chicken on a carving board and surround with fruit. Serves 6 generously. Contains about 300 calories per serving.

Lemon Marinade: Mix together ⅓ cup each lemon juice and dry white wine, 2 tablespoons olive oil, 1 teaspoon each salt and orégano, ½ teaspoon each tarragon and black pepper, and 3 cloves minced garlic.

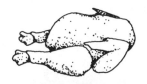

Roast Chicken Orangerie

A tantalizing orange and glazed onion sauce gilds chicken for a gala
party dish.

**3-pound broiler-fryer
salt and pepper
2 cloves garlic, minced
½ teaspoon crumbled dried tarragon
16 small boiling onions, peeled
3 tablespoons orange juice concentrate, thawed
2 oranges, peeled and sliced
watercress or parsley for garnish**

Wash chicken and pat dry. Place in a roasting pan, sprinkle with salt
and pepper, and scatter garlic and tarragon over all. Roast in a 425°
oven for 20 minutes or until lightly browned; reduce temperature to
350° and roast 1½ hours longer. Place chicken on a platter, cover with
foil, and keep warm. Pour off the pan drippings and skim fat. If
necessary, pour ¼ cup water into the pan and scrape up drippings.
Sauté onions in 1 teaspoon of the chicken fat or margarine. Add the
chicken stock created from the drippings, cover pan, and simmer 10
minutes. Stir in the orange concentrate and heat until blended. Carve
chicken into serving portions and spoon over the onions and sauce.
Arrange a few orange slices alongside. Garnish with watercress.
Makes 4 to 6 servings. Contains about 275 to 325 calories per serving.

Roast Chicken and Vegetables

Cook the vegetables in the pan juices as the bird "sets up," ready for carving.

3-pound broiler-fryer
1 teaspoon each salt and crumbled dried orégano
freshly ground pepper
3 cloves garlic, minced
¼ cup lemon juice
½ cup water
½ pound button mushrooms
1½ pounds peas, shelled, or
1 package (10 ounces) frozen petit peas, thawed

Rub chicken with salt, orégano, and pepper, and sprinkle with garlic. Place on a rack in a roasting pan and roast in a 425° oven for 30 minutes, or until golden brown. Reduce heat to 325° and continue roasting 1 hour longer. Remove from oven, pour lemon juice over chicken, transfer to a hot platter, and cover loosely with foil. Skim fat from the pan drippings and stir in water. Bring to a boil, add mushrooms and peas, and simmer until hot through. Carve chicken and serve vegetables and juices alongside. Serves 4 to 6. Contains 200 to 250 calories per serving.

Chicken Jerusalem

Of the countless versions of this popular chicken and artichoke
casserole, this one is a stand-out.

4 large split chicken breasts
salt, paprika, and pepper to taste
⅛ teaspoon each crumbled dried tarragon and rosemary
1½ teaspoons butter
¼ pound small fresh mushrooms
1½ tablespoons lemon juice
⅓ cup dry white wine
1 tablespoon Sherry
1 teaspoon chicken stock base
1 package (8 ounces) frozen artichoke hearts, parboiled
finely chopped parsley

Season chicken breasts with salt, paprika, pepper, tarragon, and
rosemary. Place in a shallow baking dish and bake in a 375° oven for
20 minutes, or until cooked through. Using a large frying pan, melt
butter and sauté mushrooms with lemon juice until glazed. Add wine,
Sherry, chicken stock base, and cooked artichoke hearts and heat
through. Spoon vegetables over the chicken and quickly boil down
remaining juices until slightly reduced and spoon over all. Sprinkle
with parsley. Serves 4. Contains about 200 calories per serving.

Stir-Fry Chicken and Vegetables ✓

Once everything is assembled, you can stir-fry this Oriental medley in minutes. Offer egg flower soup as a first course, and a dessert of tangerines or melon.　*very Good*

4 split chicken breasts (about 1⅓ pounds)
½ teaspoon cornstarch
1 tablespoon peanut or safflower oil
½ teaspoon salt
½ cup chicken stock
¼ pound mushrooms, sliced
1 small can (4 ounces) bamboo shoots, thinly sliced
¼ pound edible pea pods
dash white pepper
2 teaspoons soy sauce
½ teaspoon sugar
3 drops sesame oil
1½ teaspoons cornstarch dissolved in 1 tablespoon cold water

Skin chicken and remove meat from bones; slice wafer thin, then cut into 1½-inch squares. Toss in the cornstarch. Heat a wok or frying pan, add oil, salt, and chicken and, stirring, cook over high heat 1 minute, or until chicken turns white. Add stock, mushrooms, bamboo shoots, and pea pods. Cover pan and cook 1½ minutes. Add pepper, soy sauce, sugar, sesame oil, and cornstarch mixture. Cook, stirring, until thickened. Serves 4. Contains 220 calories per serving.

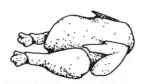

Good

Tarragon Chicken and Vegetables

An herb-flavored wine sauce gilds chicken, onions, and mushrooms in this make-ahead chicken stew.

1 each carrot and onion, chopped
1 tablespoon butter
1 broiler-fryer, cut-up (about 3 pounds) or chicken breasts, thighs, and drumsticks
½ pound small whole mushrooms
¾ cup dry white wine
½ cup chicken broth
1/2-1 teaspoon each salt and tarragon
¾ pound small boiling onions, peeled and parboiled, or
1 package (10 ounces) frozen boiling onions, thawed

Using a large dutch oven or flame-proof casserole, sauté carrot and onion in butter until glazed; push to the sides of the pan. Add chicken pieces and brown on all sides. Add mushrooms to pan and sauté quickly in drippings. Add wine, broth, salt, tarragon, and onions. Bake in a 375° oven for 45 minutes or until chicken is just tender, basting once or twice with pan juices. Makes 4 to 6 servings. Contains about 250 to 300 calories per serving.

Greek Roast Turkey

Herbs and lemon juice imbue the bird with an evocative fragrance.

20-pound turkey
salt and pepper
1/3 cup lemon juice
4 cloves garlic, minced
2 teaspoons crumbled dried orégano

Wash turkey thoroughly and wipe dry. Rub the entire surface as well as the cavity with salt and pepper and a few tablespoons of the lemon juice. Scatter garlic over surface and tuck inside the cavity. Place on a rack in a shallow roasting pan and insert meat thermometer in the thickest part of the thigh. Roast in a 425° oven for 40 minutes; reduce temperature to 325° and roast until thermometer registers 175°, about 4 to 4½ hours. Sprinkle with orégano and pour remaining lemon juice over all. Transfer to a carving board. Pour ½ cup water into pan drippings and bring to a boil; skim fat and serve alongside. Makes about 20 servings. Figure about 200 calories per 4-ounce serving.

Greek Roast Chicken Variation: Wash a 3-pound broiler-fryer and pat dry. Season with salt and pepper and sprinkle with 2 cloves garlic, minced. Place on a rack and roast in a 425° oven for 20 minutes; reduce heat to 325° and roast 1½ hours longer, or until drumstick moves easily. Pour over 3 tablespoons lemon juice and sprinkle with ½ teaspoon crumbled dried orégano. Pour ¼ cup water into pan drippings and bring to a boil; skim fat and serve juices alongside.

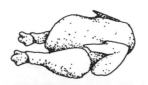

Vegetable Stuffing

Basil and Romano cheese punctuate this greens and beef stuffing. Let it accompany roast turkey.

½ loaf French bread (12 slices)
2 eggs
1 cup chicken or turkey broth
1 onion, chopped
1 tablespoon whipped margarine
1 bunch Swiss chard, chopped
1 stalk celery, chopped
1 pound ground veal or beef
2 teaspoons salt
3 tablespoons fresh chopped basil or pesto sauce
¼ teaspoon each sage and rosemary
¾ cup grated Romano cheese
¾ cup chopped parsley

Slice bread ½ inch thick and cut in cubes. Beat eggs and broth and pour over bread. Sauté onion in margarine until limp; add chard and celery and sauté until glazed. Remove to a bowl. Brown meat, season with salt, basil, sage, and rosemary and mix with vegetables. Add bread, ½ cup of the cheese, and parsley. Spoon into a shallow casserole or baking dish and sprinkle with remaining cheese. Bake at 375° for 30 to 40 minutes or until slightly browned. Makes enough stuffing to serve 10 to 12. Contains about 150 calories per serving.

Keftethes (Garlic Turkey Patties)

Ground dark turkey meat is the surprising base for these flavor-packed little meatballs, finished off with a concentrated vinegar sauce.

1 pound ground dark turkey meat
2 egg whites
¼ cup nonfat dry milk solids
2 cloves garlic, minced
2 shallots or green onions, chopped
¼ cup finely chopped parsley
1 teaspoon salt
¼ teaspoon each pepper and orégano
1½ teaspoons butter or oil or nonstick pan
3 tablespoons red-wine vinegar

Mix together the ground meat, egg whites, milk solids, garlic, shallots, parsley, salt, pepper, and orégano. Shape into oval patties, about ½ inch thick. Brown in butter or in a nonstick pan, turning to brown both sides and cooking until no longer pink inside. Pour in vinegar and cook down, scraping up drippings. Makes 4 servings. Contains 270 calories per serving.

Oriental Meatballs

Here turkey substitutes for pork in gingered meatballs, with water chestnuts providing a delightful crunch.

1 pound raw ground turkey
2 egg whites
6 tablespoons chopped water chestnuts
1 tablespoon each soy sauce and pale dry Sherry
2 cloves garlic, minced
¾ teaspoon salt
2 slices freshly chopped ginger
2 teaspoons cornstarch
½ tablespoon whipped margarine
special sauce: see below

For meatballs, mix together the turkey, egg whites, water chestnuts, soy sauce, Sherry, garlic, salt, ginger, and cornstarch. Shape into 1½-inch balls for entrée-size servings or ¾-inch balls for appetizers. Brown in margarine in a large frying pan, turning to brown on all sides. Transfer to a shallow baking dish. Pour Special Sauce over it and bake in a 350° oven for 10 minutes. Makes 4 entrée servings or 30 appetizer servings. Contains about 235 calories per entrée serving and 30 calories per appetizer serving.

Special Sauce: Mix together 3 tablespoons unsweetened pineapple juice or apple juice, 1 tablespoon soy sauce, 1½ tablespoons catsup, 2 teaspoons vinegar, 1 clove minced garlic, a few drops sesame oil, and 1 slice freshly chopped ginger.

Meats

An international feeling envelops this entrée section. And for me, each dish elicits fond memories . . .

In the walled town of Dubrovnik at a courtyard restaurant we savored anise-scented Yugoslavian Cabbage Rolls, each deliciously caramelized after hours of gentle cooking. Amid the polished ambience of a centuries-old Amsterdam canal home we sampled Dutch Cordon Bleu, tender steak plumped with choice Gouda and lean ham. The Turkish-Slashed Eggplant dish stems from a petite Istanbul matron, quite at home visiting in a California kitchen. Greece and its sunny isles abound in variations of *Moussaka*; this one is from a seaport resort on Crete. In late springtime, a favored Milanese luncheon is first-of-the-season asparagus baked with eggs and Parmesan. Steak with Green Peppercorn Sauce typifies the good French way little bistros turn out a pan-fried steak. And *Köfte* brings remembrances of Gelik, a seaport restaurant in Turkey where grilled lamb was never better.

Preference is given here to the leaner cuts of meat: veal, leg of lamb, round steak, and rump roast. One hint for making very thin meat slices for sukiyaki or *spiedini* dishes: place the roast or steak in the freezer for about half an hour before slicing. When frosty and firm, it slices with ease.

Dutch Cordon Bleu

The classic French way of stuffing veal with ham and Gruyère receives many variations throughout the Continent. Beef is often substituted for veal, along with local cheese and ham.

1 pound top sirloin or round steak, cut in 4 servings or boneless veal steak or cutlets
salt and pepper to taste
2 ounces Gouda or Gruyère cheese
4 slices boiled ham or proscuitto
1 teaspoon butter or margarine
¼ cup beef stock
1 tablespoon red-wine vinegar
1 tablespoon each chopped parsley and chives

Cut a pocket in one side of each steak, making an opening to within ½ inch of the other three sides. Season meat with salt and pepper. Slip a slice of cheese and ham inside each steak pocket. Heat a large frying pan; add butter and steak. Pan fry until browned; then turn and brown other side. Remove to a platter and keep warm. Add stock and vinegar and cook down until slightly reduced. Add parsley and chives and spoon over meat. Makes 4 servings. Contains about 340 calories per serving with beef or 250 calories per serving with veal.

Steak with Green Peppercorn Sauce

The little green peppercorns lend a fiery pizzazz to a smooth mustard
sauce on steak.

1½ pounds top round or sirloin
1 teaspoon butter
2 tablespoons brandy
1 shallot, minced
2 teaspoons green peppercorns, rinsed
¼ cup each rich beef or chicken stock and dry white wine
2 tablespoons heavy cream
1 tablespoon Dijon-style mustard
½ teaspoon crumbled dried tarragon
salt and pepper to taste

Using a large frying pan, sauté meat in butter until browned, turning to
cook both sides and cooking until medium rare. Ignite brandy and pour
flaming over the meat. Remove to a carving board. Add shallot,
peppercorns, stock, wine, cream, mustard, and tarragon and cook
down juices until slightly reduced. Slice steak into strips and place on
a hot platter; spoon sauce over it. Makes 6 servings. Contains about
290 calories per serving.

Steak and Mushrooms Dijon

Utilizing French seasonings instead of Oriental ones, here is a quick stir-fry entrée made with beef and mushrooms.

¼ pound mushrooms, thinly sliced
1 tablespoon butter or margarine
1 clove garlic, minced
1 pound beefsteak, very thinly sliced into strips as for sukiyaki (flank or round steak are suitable)
1 tablespoon cornstarch
salt and pepper to taste
⅓ cup each dry red wine and beef broth
1 teaspoon Dijon-style mustard
½ teaspoon anchovy paste
1 tablespoon each minced parsley and chives or green onions

Using a large frying pan or wok, quickly sauté mushrooms in 1 teaspoon butter with garlic, stirring constantly, just until heated through; turn out onto a serving platter. Dip meat in a mixture of cornstarch, salt, and pepper and stir-fry in remaining butter, doing half of the meat at a time, just until browned on both sides; transfer to a serving platter. Pour into the pan drippings the wine and broth and cook down until reduced by half. Stir in mustard and anchovy paste. Cook, stirring until blended. Return meat and mushrooms to the pan and stir just to coat. Turn onto the platter and sprinkle with parsley and chives. Serves 4. Contains about 275 calories per serving.

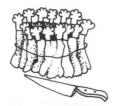

Moroccan Beef and Pear Tajine

A conical pot, called a *tajine,* is used for cooking Moroccan meat and fruit stews. The delightful mélange of spices, honey, citrus, and nuts provides a beautiful union of flavors.

1 large onion, chopped
1½ teaspoons shredded fresh ginger root
1 teaspoon salt
freshly ground pepper
⅛ teaspoon turmeric
1 stick cinnamon
½ teaspoon butter
2 cloves garlic, minced
2 pounds lean beef stew, cut in 1½-inch cubes
8 dried pear halves
1 tablespoon honey
1½ tablespoons lime or lemon juice
2 tablespoons chopped pistachios or toasted almonds
1 tablespoon chopped cilantro (optional)
lime or lemon wedges

In a heavy dutch oven sauté onion, ginger, salt, pepper, turmeric, and cinnamon in butter until glazed. Add garlic and beef and sauté a few minutes. Cover and bake in a 325° oven for 1½ hours. Cut pears into thirds, add to meat, and bake 30 minutes longer, or until tender. Add honey and lime juice to pan drippings and heat, scraping up drippings. Sprinkle with nuts and cilantro and garnish with lime wedges. Serves 8. Contains about 275 calories per serving.

Veal and Apricot Variation: Substitute 2 pounds veal stew meat or calf for the beef and 16 apricots for the pears, if desired. Contains about 225 calories per serving.

Lamb and Prune Variation: Substitute 2 pounds lamb stew meat for the beef and 16 prunes for the pears. Contains about 275 calories per serving.

Sukiyaki

This is a congenial entrée to cook at the table before guests. In fact, they may participate.

1 pound top round steak or flank steak
1 bunch green onions
4 or 5 stalks celery
¼ pound mushrooms, sliced
1 can (4 ounces) water chestnuts, drained and sliced
1 pound spinach, stems removed, or broccoli, sliced diagonally
1 pound bean sprouts
½ cup each soy sauce and beef stock
2 tablespoons sugar
1 tablespoon peanut or safflower oil

Slice meat across the grain into ⅛-inch thick slices. Trim ends from green onions and slice lengthwise, then cut crosswise into 1½-inch strips. Slice celery diagonally into ½-inch pieces. Arrange meat and vegetables on a tray in individual mounds. Mix together soy sauce, stock, and sugar. Using a wok or large frying pan, prepare half the sukiyaki at a time. Heat half the oil, add half the meat, and cook until browned. Add half the celery and broccoli (if used) and the soy mixture and cook 5 minutes. Add half the onions, mushrooms, water chestnuts, spinach, and bean sprouts and heat through. Repeat with second batch. Makes 4 servings. Contains about 310 calories per serving.

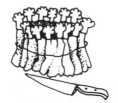

Roast with Shallot Sauce

A rich glaze of shallots and wine cloaks slices of roast beef.

3- to 4-pound sirloin tip or cross rib roast
salt and pepper
3 cloves garlic
½ cup minced shallots
1 tablespoon butter
¾ cup dry red wine and beef stock
2 tablespoons minced parsley

Season meat with salt and pepper to taste and stud with split, peeled garlic cloves. Roast in a 325° oven until meat thermometer registers rare. Reserve drippings and skim fat. Meanwhile sauté shallots in 1 teaspoon of the butter until glazed. Add wine and stock and cook down until reduced by half. Stir in remaining drippings, butter, and parsley. Slice meat and spoon a little sauce over each serving. Makes 10 to 12 servings. Contains about 275 calories per serving.

Beef Birds Spiedini

Skewered pinwheels of steak barbecue to succulence as the cheese melts within.

1 pound thinly sliced steak or roast, cut ¼-inch thick: see below
salt, garlic salt, and fresh ground pepper to taste
½ teaspoon crumbled dried orégano
1 ounce very thinly sliced proscuitto or Black Forest ham
2 ounces Gruyère, Samsoe, or Fontinella cheese

Cut meat slices into 3-by-5-inch rectangles. Sprinkle with salt, garlic salt, pepper, and orégano. Lay a small piece of proscuitto and cheese on each meat strip and roll up. Skewer. Repeat, skewering about 4 meat rolls on each skewer. Barbecue or broil over hot coals, turning. Makes 4 servings. Contains about 270 calories per serving.

Note: A roast such as a sirloin tip, rump, or cross rib is excellent for slicing into wafer-thin steak strips. As an aid, place the roast in the freezer for about 1 hour to firm it up before slicing.

Beef Roll Italian Style

This meat roll encloses a bright green stuffing that has Italian sausage threading its center.

2 pounds top round, butterflied
3 tablespoons Dijon-style mustard
2 or 3 Italian sausages
1 bunch green onions, chopped
2 teaspoons butter or margarine
1 bunch fresh spinach, finely chopped
2 cloves garlic, minced
2 tablespoons chopped parsley
1 tablespoon chopped fresh basil or ½ teaspoon dried basil
1 egg
½ teaspoon salt
⅓ cup shredded Parmesan or Romano cheese
1 medium-sized onion, finely chopped
1 carrot, peeled and chopped
¼ cup dry white wine

Lay open the steak on a board, cover with a sheet of waxed paper, and pound lightly until of even thickness. Spread with mustard. Place sausage in a saucepan, cover with water, bring to a boil, and simmer very gently for 15 minutes; drain. Using a large frying pan, sauté green onions in 1 teaspoon of the butter until limp. Add spinach and cook until barely wilted. Turn into a bowl. Mix in garlic, parsley, basil, egg, salt, and cheese. Spread the spinach filling over the mustard-coated meat. Lay sausages in a ribbon down the center. Roll up and tie with a string. Place on a baking pan. Meanwhile sauté onion and carrot in remaining butter until glazed and spoon around the meat roll. Bake in a 425° oven for 20 minutes. Pour wine into pan and continue baking 5 to 10 minutes longer, or until steak is browned but still slightly pink inside. Cut into 1-inch slices and spoon vegetable sauce alongside. Makes 8 servings. Contains about 330 calories per serving.

Stir-Fry Broccoli and Beef

Complement this fast Oriental dish with another, such as Shrimp and Snow Peas, for a complete dinner entrée.

½ pound flank steak, thinly sliced
2 teaspoons soy sauce
1 teaspoon sugar
1 clove garlic, minced
2 slices ginger root
3 tablespoons Vermouth or dry white wine
1 tablespoon cornstarch
1 tablespoon oil
½ teaspoon salt
1 small bunch broccoli, stems peeled and flowerets cut diagonally into
bite-sized pieces
1 onion, cut into sections

Marinate meat in a mixture of soy sauce, sugar, garlic, ginger root, 1 tablespoon of the Vermouth, and the cornstarch. Add half the oil and the salt to a very hot wok or frying pan, and stir-fry broccoli and onion, stirring constantly, until broccoli turns greener, about 1 to 2 minutes. Add remaining 2 tablespoons wine, cover, and cook over high heat for 5 minutes. Turn out onto a platter with the flowerets pointing outward.

Heat remaining oil in wok and cook marinated beef, stirring constantly, for 1 to 2 minutes. Turn out onto the center of the broccoli. Makes 4 servings, but include another protein-rich dish for a complete entrée. Contains about 140 calories per serving.

Korean Steak Strips Teriyaki

Interweave soy-glazed flank steak strips between onion and pepper on skewers for a succulent barbecued entrée.

1 flank steak (about 1½ pounds)
½ teaspoon each salt and monosodium glutamate
2 tablespoons soy sauce
2 teaspoons sugar
1 clove garlic, minced
freshly ground pepper
1 green onion, chopped
1 tablespoon sesame oil
1 onion, peeled
1 green pepper

Slice steak into strips about ⅜ inch wide and 6 inches long. Marinate meat in a mixture of the salt, monosodium glutamate, soy sauce, sugar, garlic, pepper, chopped onion, and oil for 30 minutes to 1 hour. Cut onion into ½-inch wedges. Cut peppers in half and remove seeds. Cut into large pieces. Thread each steak strip on a skewer at 1-inch intervals and add a piece of onion and green pepper at each end. Barbecue over charcoal or under a broiler, turning to brown both sides. Makes 6 servings. Contains 280 calories per serving.

Asparagus Beef

When fresh asparagus has its brief turn in the marketplace, this is a delightful Oriental way to serve it.

1 small flank steak, cut into ⅛-inch-thick strips (about 1 pound)
1 teaspoon salt
1 teaspoon cornstarch
2 teaspoons soy sauce
1½ pounds asparagus
1 medium-sized onion
2 tablespoons peanut or safflower oil
2 cloves garlic, minced
3 tablespoons canned bean sauce
½ teaspoon sugar

Place meat in a bowl with ½ teaspoon salt, cornstarch, and soy sauce. Snap off the tough ends of the asparagus and cut diagonally into ¼-inch-thick pieces. Cut onion in half lengthwise, then slice crosswise into ¼-inch slices. Heat a wok or frying pan and add 1 tablespoon oil. Add garlic and cook until light brown. Remove and discard. Add meat, stir, and cook until almost browned. Remove to a bowl. Add remaining oil and onion. Cook a minute, stirring. Stir in bean sauce. Add asparagus, ½ teaspoon salt, sugar, and 1 tablespoon soy sauce. Cover and cook until asparagus is crisp tender. Add meat and reheat. Serves 4. Contains about 290 calories per serving.

Turkish-Slashed Eggplant

The slender, small Japanese eggplants work beautifully for this dish.
Long baking produces a smooth caramelized flavor.

2 medium-sized onions
1 teaspoon olive oil
1 pound lean ground beef chuck or round
3 medium-sized tomatoes
3 tablespoons chopped parsley
1 teaspoon salt
freshly ground pepper
2 cloves garlic, minced
¼ teaspoon allspice
8 Japanese eggplants or 2 small regular eggplants, cut in 4 wedges each
¼ cup shredded Romano cheese
½ cup tomato sauce

Sauté onions in oil until golden. Add beef and cook until browned. Peel
and chop tomatoes and add along with parsley, salt, pepper, garlic, and
allspice. Cover and simmer 10 minutes. Slit eggplant lengthwise to
within 1 inch of ends. Sprinkle with salt and set aside for 20 minutes.
Wash eggplant, pat dry, and place in a baking pan. Cover with foil and
bake in a 400° oven for 30 minutes. Remove from oven and fill each
slash with stuffing. Slice remaining tomato and garnish top of
eggplant. Sprinkle with cheese. Pour tomato sauce around eggplant.
Cover with foil and bake in a 375° oven for 1 hour. Uncover and broil 1
minute. Serve hot or warm. Serves 4. Contains about 310 calories per
serving.

Grilled Hamburgers with Herbs

A fresh herb dressing coats hamburgers for a zesty taste.

1 pound lean ground round
1 egg or 2 egg whites
1 shallot or green onion, chopped
1 clove garlic, minced
2 tablespoons chopped parsley
salt
herb dressing: see below

Mix meat with egg, shallot, garlic, and parsley. Shape into 4 patties. Sprinkle salt lightly in a large frying pan and sauté patties over moderately high heat, turning to brown both sides and cooking until medium rare. Transfer to a platter and spoon over Herb Dressing. Makes 4 servings. Contains about 245 calories per serving.

Herb Dressing: In a bowl mix together ¼ cup chopped parsley, 2 chopped shallots or green onions, 1 clove minced garlic, ½ teaspoon crumbled dried orégano, and 2 tablespoons lemon juice.

Steak Tartar

This entrée is fun to serve. You might round out the menu with Wine Broth with Pesto, Cold Artichokes Piquant, and cheese and fruit.

1 pound very lean ground sirloin or top round
1 egg or 2 egg whites
1 teaspoon salt
1½ teaspoons each Worcestershire and Dijon-style mustard
1 tablespoon red-wine vinegar
2 green onions or shallots, finely chopped (white part only)
1 tablespoon chopped parsley
1 clove garlic, minced
freshly ground pepper
watercress
cherry tomatoes
capers

Place ground meat, the egg or egg whites, salt, Worcestershire, mustard, vinegar, onions, parsley, garlic, and pepper in a mixing bowl and mix until blended. Shape into 4 patties. Place each on a bed of watercress and ring with cherry tomatoes. Scatter a few capers over the tomatoes. Makes 4 servings. Contains about 290 calories per serving.

Ground Round Mexicali

Fresh sliced pineapple and green *chile* peppers underlie the broiled cheese topping on these exceptional hamburgers.

1 medium-sized onion, chopped
½ teaspoon whipped margarine
1 pound ground sirloin or round
salt and pepper
2 tablespoons diced canned green chile peppers
4 thin slices fresh pineapple
2 ounces sliced Monterey Jack or Gruyère cheese
4 canned red sweet peppers

Sauté onion in margarine until limp and golden brown, cooking slowly. Shape meat into 4 patties and season with salt and pepper. Place on a broiling pan and broil until browned on both sides, cooking until medium rare. Remove from the oven and distribute onion and *chile* peppers over them. Top with a slice of pineapple and the cheese. Return to the oven and broil until cheese melts. Top each patty with a red pepper. Makes 4 servings. Contains about 300 calories per serving.

Moussaka

The celebrated Middle East eggplant casserole lends itself to a slim version as well.

1 pound lean ground beef or lamb
1 large onion, chopped
1 teaspoon salt
1 clove garlic, minced
1 can (6 ounces) tomato paste
1 teaspoon mixed pickling spice
2 tablespoons red-wine vinegar
2 tablespoons minced parsley
3 cups low-fat milk
3 tablespoons cornstarch blended with 3 tablespoons cold water
¾ teaspoon salt
⅛ teaspoon nutmeg
1 large eggplant, sliced ½-inch thick
3 eggs
⅓ cup grated Parmesan cheese

Sauté meat and onion in a heavy frying pan, stirring until crumbly. Add salt, garlic, tomato paste, mixed pickling spice tied in a cheesecloth bag, vinegar, parsley, and about ½ cup water. Cover and simmer 3 hours. Skim off fat. Heat milk until scalded and blend in the cornstarch paste. Cook, stirring, until thickened. Season with salt and nutmeg. Meanwhile lay out eggplant on a sheet of foil in a baking pan and bake in a 400° oven for 30 minutes, turning once. Using a greased 9-by-13-inch baking pan, arrange eggplant in a layer on the bottom and cover with meat sauce. Stir thickened milk into beaten eggs and pour over the top. Sprinkle with cheese. Bake in a 350° oven for 45 minutes, or until set and browned. Cut into squares. Makes about 9 servings. Contains about 200 calories per serving.

Köfte

Diamond-shaped meat patties, studded with melted nuggets of Gruyère, are a favorite barbecue entrée in Turkey. For variation, ground veal may replace the lamb.

¾ pound each lean ground beef and lamb or veal
2 green onions, chopped (white part only)
1 tablespoon chopped parsley
1½ teaspoons salt
freshly ground pepper
¼ teaspoon each ground cumin and crumbled dried orégano
2 cloves garlic, minced
¾ cup (3 ounces) finely diced Gruyère or Norwegian Jarlsberg cheese
(cut in ¼-inch square pieces)
6 tablespoons low-fat yogurt
2 teaspoons chopped green onion tops or chives

Place in a mixing bowl the ground meats, onions, parsley, salt, pepper, cumin, orégano, and garlic. Mix thoroughly. Mix in the cheese until well distributed. Form meat into six diamond-shaped patties, each about 5½ inches long and 3½ inches across. Barbecue over medium-hot coals or broil, turning to brown both sides and allowing about 3 minutes on a side for medium-rare. Serve accompanied by a bowl of yogurt blended with green onions to spoon over. Makes 6 servings. Contains about 310 calories per serving.

Joe's Special

An old-time specialty from New Joe's North Beach Italian Restaurant in San Francisco, this scramble of beef, spinach, and egg is a fine spur-of-the-moment entrée.

2 green onions, chopped
¼ pound mushrooms, sliced
1 teaspoon butter or margarine
1 pound lean ground calf or beef
2 cloves garlic, minced
1 teaspoon salt
pepper to taste
1 bunch spinach, finely chopped
2 eggs
3 tablespoons shredded Romano or Parmesan cheese

Using a large frying pan or wok, sauté onions and mushrooms in butter just until glazed. Push to sides of pan, add ground meat, garlic, salt, and pepper and cook until browned. Mix in spinach and cook for 2 minutes, just until spinach wilts. Break eggs over the mixture and stir with a fork to mix in and cook through. Sprinkle with cheese. Serves 4. Contains about 270 calories per serving.

Mushroom-Capped Hamburgers

A broiled blue cheese dressing and sautéed mushrooms smother grilled hamburgers.

2 ounces blue cheese
¼ cup low-fat yogurt
1 green onion, chopped
2 tablespoons chopped parsley
1 onion, finely chopped
1 tablespoon whipped margarine
½ pound mushrooms, sliced
1 pound ground round or sirloin
salt and pepper

Beat together the cheese, yogurt, green onion, and parsley; set aside. Sauté onion in half the margarine until limp. Add mushrooms and remaining margarine and sauté just until hot through; set aside. Shape meat into 4 patties and place on a broiling rack. Season with salt and pepper and broil, turning to brown both sides, and cooking until medium-rare. Spoon mushrooms over each patty and top with a dollop of cheese dressing. Return to the broiler just until cheese browns lightly. Makes 4 servings. Contains about 310 calories per serving.

Veal Steaks Oscar

A Scandinavian specialty pairs veal with seafood for an elegant, eye-pleasing entrée.

1 pound boneless veal cutlets or steak, cut ⅜-inch thick
salt and pepper to taste
¼ teaspoon dried tarragon
1½ teaspoons butter
2 tablespoons dry white wine or Vermouth
12 medium-sized cooked shrimp or ¼ pound small cooked shrimp
1 package (8 ounces) frozen artichoke hearts, cooked, or ¾ pound fresh asparagus, cooked
low-calorie béarnaise sauce: see page 4

Cut meat into serving-size pieces, place between sheets of waxed paper, and pound lightly. Season meat with salt, pepper, and tarragon and sauté in 1 teaspoon butter in a large frying pan, turning to brown both sides. Add wine, cover, and simmer 5 to 10 minutes, or until meat is tender. Heat shrimp in remaining butter. Arrange meat on a platter or individual plates and place several artichoke hearts or asparagus spears on top of each steak. Scatter shrimp on top and pour hot Low-Calorie Béarnaise Sauce over all. Makes 4 servings. Contains 300 calories per serving.

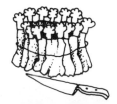

Veal Stroganoff

Yogurt makes a creamy substitute for sour cream in this Russian-style entrée.

1 tablespoon butter or oil
¼ pound mushrooms, sliced
1 onion, finely chopped
1 pound veal loin, cut in ½-inch strips
1 teaspoon salt
1 clove garlic, minced
1 cup beef or chicken stock
1 tablespoon tomato paste
1 teaspoon Worcestershire
½ teaspoon dry mustard
dash Angostura bitters
1 tablespoon cornstarch
2 tablespoons dry Sherry
⅓ cup low-fat yogurt
watercress for garnish

Heat half the butter in a large frying pan and sauté mushrooms until glazed. Turn out of pan and set aside. Sauté onion and veal in remaining butter until meat is browned. Add the salt, garlic, stock, tomato paste, Worcestershire, mustard, and bitters. Cover and simmer 30 minutes, or until meat is tender. Stir in a paste of cornstarch and Sherry and cook until thickened. Mix in yogurt and mushrooms and heat through. Garnish with watercress. Makes 4 servings. Contains about 250 calories per serving.

Veal Roast with Onion Sauce

A smothering of caramelized onions enhances a braised veal roast.

3-pound veal roast
1 teaspoon salt
freshly ground pepper
2 cloves garlic, minced
½ teaspoon crumbled dried marjoram
1 tablespoon olive oil
3 onions, sliced
½ cup dry white wine
¼ cup lemon juice
1 cup beef stock
bouquet garni: bay leaf, parsley sprig, a few celery leaves
1 tablespoon soy sauce
1 teaspoon Worcestershire

Season meat with salt, pepper, garlic, and marjoram. Brown in half the oil in a dutch oven. Remove from pan and set aside. Cook onions in remaining oil until limp and golden, stirring. Add wine, lemon juice, stock, *bouquet garni*, soy sauce, and Worcestershire. Return roast to pan. Cover and roast in a 325° oven for about 1½ hours or until a meat thermometer registers 170°. Remove to a carving board and slice. Pass sauce in a bowl. Makes 8 servings. Contains about 230 calories per 4-ounce serving.

Veal Stew Jadran

Scarlet peppers lend a bright finish to this orange-scented stew from Dubrovnik.

1 pound veal or calf stew meat, cut in 1¼-inch chunks
½ teaspoon salad oil
1 dozen small white boiling onions, peeled
2 cloves garlic, minced
1 teaspoon salt
¼ teaspoon crumbled dried thyme
⅔ cup dry white wine
1 beef bouillon cube plus ¼ cup water
1 strip orange zest
2 tablespoons tomato paste
1 small red pepper, seeded and diced

Using a frying pan or dutch oven, brown meat in oil, turning to brown all sides. Add onions and cook until glazed. Add garlic, salt, thyme, wine, bouillon cube, water, orange zest, and tomato paste. Cover and simmer 1¼ hours or until meat is tender. Spoon into ramekins and sprinkle with diced pepper. Makes 4 servings. Contains about 270 calories per serving.

Veal and Mushroom Stifado

This classic Greek stew is punctuated with pickling spice and wine vinegar.

1½ pounds veal stew, cut in 1¼-inch pieces
2 teaspoons butter or oil
1½ teaspoons salt
2 cloves garlic, minced
1 teaspoon mixed pickling spice, tied in cheesecloth
1 pound small boiling onions, peeled and parboiled 2 minutes
⅓ cup each dry red wine and water
3 tablespoons red-wine vinegar
3 tablespoons tomato paste
1 teaspoon brown sugar
½ pound small mushrooms
chopped parsley

Using a dutch oven or flameproof casserole, brown meat in butter on all sides. Season with salt and garlic. Add pickling spice, onions, wine, water, vinegar, tomato paste, and sugar. Cover and simmer 1 hour, or until meat is almost tender. Add mushrooms and cook just until mushrooms are heated through. Ladle into small ramekins and garnish with parsley. Makes 6 servings. Contains about 250 calories per serving.

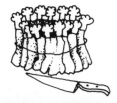

Veal Piccatta *delicious*

Lemon sparks this fast Italian-style sautéed entrée.

1 pound veal scallopini
1 tablespoon cornstarch
½ teaspoon each salt and garlic salt
freshly ground pepper
1 tablespoon butter
2 tablespoons lemon juice
¼ cup each dry white wine and beef broth
lemon slices and watercress for garnish

Dip meat in a mixture of the cornstarch, salt, garlic salt, and pepper, lightly coating both sides. Using a large frying pan, sauté meat in butter, turning to brown both sides and cooking quickly. Transfer to a platter. Pour into the pan drippings the lemon juice, wine, and broth and cook, stirring until smooth and reduced to about ¼ cup. Spoon over meat. Garnish with lemon slices and watercress. Makes 4 servings. Contains about 275 calories per serving.

Note: As a variation add 2 tablespoons large capers along with the wine and broth.

Veal Scallopini with Marsala

An economical way to acquire thin veal slices is to cut your own from a partially frozen boneless roast. This Italian dish calls for last-minute timing.

¼ pound mushrooms
1 tablespoon butter or margarine
1½ teaspoons lemon juice
1 pound veal, cut for scallopini
1 tablespoon cornstarch
½ teaspoon salt
freshly ground pepper
¼ cup Marsala or dry Sherry
½ teaspoon beef stock base dissolved in 2 tablespoons water
1 clove garlic, minced
1 tablespoon chopped parsley

Slice mushrooms thinly. Using a large frying pan, sauté mushrooms in half the butter with the lemon juice just until glazed; turn out of pan and set aside. Cut veal into 1-inch-wide strips. Mix together cornstarch, salt, and pepper and sprinkle over meat, coating evenly. Melt remaining butter and brown part of the meat at a time, cooking quickly, and turning to brown both sides. Remove to a platter. Pour in wine and beef stock. Add garlic and cook 1 minute, scraping up drippings. Return mushrooms and meat to the pan and heat through. Sprinkle with parsley. Serves 4. Contains about 250 calories per serving.

Veal with Eggplant

This Turkish meat and vegetable casserole is easily made in advance.
A salad and a fruit dessert complete the menu.

1 pound veal stew meat
salt and freshly ground pepper
1 teaspoon olive oil
2 cloves garlic, minced
3 tablespoons tomato paste
1 cup water
2 tablespoons white-wine vinegar
½ teaspoon dried thyme or tarragon
12 small white boiling onions, peeled
1 large eggplant, peeled and cut into 1-inch cubes
2 tablespoons chopped parsley
4 slices lemon

Season meat with salt and pepper and brown in oil in a heavy
flameproof casserole. Add garlic, tomato paste, water, vinegar, and
thyme. Cover and simmer 1 hour. Add onions and eggplant and
simmer 20 to 30 minutes longer, or until meat and vegetables are
tender. Sprinkle with parsley and garnish with lemon slices. Makes 4
servings. Contains 225 calories per serving.

Veal and Mushroom Strudels

Crisp filo envelops veal and mushrooms in neat cylinders.

1 medium-sized onion, chopped
3 tablespoons whipped margarine
½ pound mushrooms
1 pound ground veal
½ teaspoon each salt and crumbled dried tarragon
1 clove garlic, minced
½ cup shredded Parmesan cheese
⅓ cup chopped proscuitto or ham
1 egg
2 tablespoons chopped parsley
8 sheets prepared filo dough (about 4 ounces or ¼ package)

Using a large frying pan, sauté onion in 1 tablespoon of the margarine until golden. Add mushrooms and cook until glazed. Add veal, salt, tarragon, and garlic and cook until meat is browned. Mix in cheese, proscuitto, egg, and parsley.

Lay out 1 sheet filo, brush short half of it lightly with melted margarine and brush again with margarine. Spoon a ribbon of filling (about ⅓ cup) on a narrow edge and fold in sides 1 inch. Roll up and place seam side down on a greased baking sheet. Repeat until remaining filo and filling are used, spacing rolls 1 inch apart on baking sheet. Brush top with remaining melted margarine. Bake in a 375° oven 20 minutes, or until golden. Makes 8 rolls, or 4 generous servings. Contains 150 calories per roll.

Veal Roast with Vegetable Sauce

When blended, the cooking juices and vegetables purée into a richly flavored sauce for tender sliced veal.

1 medium-sized onion, finely chopped
1 carrot, chopped
1 teaspoon olive oil
3-pound veal roast, boned, rolled, and tied
salt and pepper
3 cloves minced garlic
1 bay leaf
1 sprig parsley
½ teaspoon crumbled dried tarragon
1 cup rich chicken stock
3 tablespoons white-wine vinegar

Using a large dutch oven, sauté onion and carrot in oil until limp. Push to the sides of the pan. Season meat with salt and pepper and brown all sides. Add garlic, bay leaf, parsley, tarragon, chicken stock, and vinegar. Cover and simmer 1½ to 2 hours, or until tender. Remove meat to a platter. Discard bay leaf and purée juices and vegetables in a blender. Reheat sauce and cook down slightly, if desired. Slice meat and ladle sauce over it. Makes 8 to 10 servings. Contains about 225 calories per serving.

Yugoslavian Cabbage Rolls

A quartet of spices season the cheese filling that goes inside these compact cabbage-leaf rolls.

1 large head cabbage (about 2 pounds)
2 medium-sized onions, finely chopped
1 teaspoon butter or margarine
¾ pound each ground veal and ground turkey
1½ teaspoons salt
½ teaspoon each ground allspice and anise seed
¼ teaspoon each ground cinnamon and freshly ground nutmeg
2 cloves garlic, minced
¾ cup low-fat cottage cheese
2 egg whites
1 can (6 ounces) tomato paste
1 cup dry red wine
1 can (1 pound) sauerkraut

Core cabbage, separate leaves, and cook in a large pot of boiling salted water until leaves are tender, about 5 to 7 minutes; drain and cool. Sauté onions in butter until glazed. Mix together the meats, salt, allspice, anise seed, cinnamon, nutmeg, garlic, cottage cheese, egg whites, and onions. Lay out a cabbage leaf and spoon a walnut-sized mound of meat at one end. Fold up sides and roll up. Combine tomato paste and wine and spoon a thin layer in two 7-by-12-inch baking dishes. Cover with the cabbage rolls. Drain sauerkraut and rinse under cold water. Combine remaining tomato paste and wine mixture with sauerkraut and spoon over the top. Cover with foil and bake in a 350° oven for 50 minutes. Makes 30 rolls, about 10 servings. Contains about 200 calories per serving.

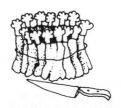

Cannelloni-Style Crêpes

Cornstarch crêpes make a tender wrapper for a veal, turkey, and ricotta stuffing. These filled or unfilled crêpes freeze well.

1 large onion, chopped
1 tablespoon whipped margarine
1 pound each ground veal or calf and ground turkey
3 cloves garlic, minced
1 pint ricotta cheese
¾ cup grated Parmesan cheese
2 eggs
1½ teaspoons salt
1 package (10 ounces) frozen chopped spinach, thawed and squeezed dry
3 tablespoons minced parsley
3 dozen crêpes: see page 76

Sauté onion in margarine until golden. Add veal, turkey, and garlic and cook until meat is browned. Mix together the ricotta, ½ cup of the Parmesan, eggs, salt, spinach, parsley, and the browned meat. To assemble, place about ⅓ cup of filling in a ribbon on each crêpe. Roll up to enclose. Place in a baking pan. Sprinkle with remaining Parmesan. Bake in a 425° oven for 10 to 12 minutes, or until heated through. Makes 3 dozen filled crêpes, or 18 servings. Contains about 135 calories per serving.

Plump-Stuffed Mushrooms

The wonderfully oversized mushrooms (about 3 to 4 inches across)
offer flavor-packed containers for a sautéed veal stuffing.

About 16 big mushroom caps, 3 to 4 inches in diameter
1 small onion, peeled and chopped
1 carrot, peeled and grated
2 teaspoons butter
2 tablespoons minced parsley
1 clove garlic, minced
¾ pound ground veal
¾ teaspoon salt
¼ teaspoon nutmeg
¼ cup chopped proscuitto or ham
3 tablespoons fine dry bread crumbs
½ cup freshly shredded Parmesan cheese
½ cup chicken broth

Remove stems from mushrooms and chop. Sauté onion and carrot in 1
teaspoon of the butter until limp; add chopped mushrooms and sauté
just until heated through. Remove to a bowl and mix in parsley and
garlic. Sauté veal in remaining butter, season with salt and nutmeg,
and add to vegetables. Mix in proscuitto, crumbs, and cheese.
Lightly pack into mushroom caps. Arrange in a baking dish and pour in
broth. Bake in a 375° oven for 25 minutes, or until mushrooms are
cooked through and filling is lightly browned. Serves 4. Contains about
190 calories per serving.

Puffed Quiche Sans Crust

This oven egg dish puffs up like an oversized mushroom cap with a golden-brown crustiness. It cuts into neat serving wedges.

6 eggs
¾ cup water
¼ cup nonfat dry milk solids
½ teaspoon salt
⅛ teaspoon nutmeg
1⅔ cups grated Swiss cheese
1 ounce lean proscuitto or other thinly sliced smoked ham

Beat eggs until light and stir in water, milk solids, salt, nutmeg, cheese, and ham. Turn into a lightly buttered 9-inch pie pan. Dot with butter. Bake in a 350° oven for 35 minutes or until puffed and golden brown. Cut in wedges. Serves 6. Contains about 200 calories per serving.

Skewered Lamb Kebabs

A subtle spiciness permeates lamb for this Indian-style kebab entrée.

1 medium-sized onion, quartered
2 tablespoons lemon juice
⅔ cup water
8 each whole cloves, peppercorns, and allspice
2 cloves garlic, minced
2 pounds boneless lamb, cut in 1½-inch cubes

Purée the onion, lemon juice, and water in a blender. Pour into a bowl and stir in cloves, peppercorns, allspice, and garlic. Add meat and marinate overnight, or at least 6 hours, turning several times. Thread on skewers. Barbecue over medium-hot coals for about 10 minutes, turning, or broil until medium-rare. Makes 8 servings. Contains about 250 calories per serving.

Lamb and Eggplant Kebabs

The Middle Eastern combination of lamb and eggplant is a natural taste treat. Skewer the meat separately from the vegetables to control the cooking time with ease.

1 pound boneless lamb, cut in about 1½-inch cubes or 8 small boned lamb chops
¼ cup dry white wine
2 tablespoons lemon juice
1 clove garlic, minced
1 teaspoon crumbled fresh rosemary or ¼ teaspoon dried rosemary
salt and pepper
1 small eggplant
1 green pepper
1 onion
1 tablespoon olive oil

Marinate meat in a mixture of the wine, lemon juice, garlic, rosemary, and salt and pepper for several hours. Thread meat on a skewer. Cut eggplant into 1½-inch cubes. Halve and seed pepper and cut into 1½-inch pieces. Peel onion, cut into sixths, and separate layers. Alternate on skewers the onion, pepper, and eggplant. Add oil to remaining marinade and brush over meat and vegetables. Barbecue over medium-hot coals or broil, turning to brown both sides, cooking meat until medium-rare and vegetables until tender, about 10 to 15 minutes. Makes 4 servings. Contains about 350 calories per serving.

Roast Leg of Lamb with Herbs

Garlic, juniper berries, and fresh rosemary accent lamb in a
Provençal manner.

**4- to 5-pound leg of lamb
4 cloves garlic
6 to 8 juniper berries
salt and freshly ground pepper
2 tablespoons fresh rosemary or 1½ teaspoons dried rosemary
¼ cup gin**

Make small incisions in the lamb and insert peeled, slivered garlic
distributing it throughout the roast. Tuck in the juniper berries. Place
on a roasting pan and insert a meat thermometer. Scatter the rosemary
over the surface. Roast in a 450° oven for 20 to 25 minutes, or until
meat is browned. Reduce temperature to 325°, pour over gin, and
continue roasting until meat thermometer registers 165° for
medium-rare meat. Slice and serve with pan juices, skimmed of fat.
Makes about 8 to 10 servings. Contains about 275 calories for each
4-ounce serving.

Vegetables

International tastes have revolutionized the produce bins. Now alongside the plebian root vegetables we can find exotic Jerusalem artichokes, Japanese eggplants, Italian fennel, Chinese sugar peas, and oyster plant, to name only a few. For centuries good cooks throughout the world have devised special ways to prepare their native vegetables. Now their ways are our ways.

This repertoire includes some of the classics: Ratatouille from Provence, Spinach Ricotta Balls from Northern Italy, and a variation of my mother-in-law's Greek *Spanakopita,* or spinach pie. Many vegetable dishes are simply accompaniments. Others might stand alone as a striking first course or a gala picnic entrée: two examples are the dramatic Indian Eggplant Slices and whole-wheat crusted Italian Spinach Pie. Two versatile Oriental seasonings, sesame oil and cilantro, are presented in Asparagus Open Sesame. For drama, the Green Pea and Spinach Soufflé is spectacular when presented at the table.

Asparagus and Eggs Milanese

In fresh asparagus season this makes a regal brunch or luncheon dish.

**1 ½ pounds fresh asparagus
1 tablespoon butter or margarine
4 eggs
salt and freshly ground pepper
2 tablespoons shredded Parmesan or Romano cheese**

Trim ends from asparagus and cook in boiling salted water until tender, about 5 to 7 minutes; drain. Melt butter in a large ovenproof platter or serving dish. Break eggs onto the platter and bake in a 350° oven until whites are just set, about 8 minutes. Arrange asparagus alongside eggs, sprinkle with cheese, and continue baking until cheese melts. Makes 4 servings. Contains about 150 calories per serving.

Asparagus Open-Sesame

This Oriental dressing refreshes cold boiled artichokes as well.

1½ pounds fresh asparagus spears
2 tablespoons each lemon juice, sesame oil, and white-wine vinegar
1 tablespoon chopped cilantro
1 green onion, chopped (white part only)
dash salt and Mexican seasoning

Trim ends from asparagus and plunge into boiling salted water. Cook 2 minutes, drain, and chill. Combine lemon juice, oil, vinegar, cilantro, onion, salt, and Mexican seasoning and spoon over the asparagus. Chill thoroughly. Makes 6 servings. Contains 50 calories per serving.

Asparagus with Sabayon Sauce

This fluffy wine sauce uplifts fresh cooked vegetables, such as asparagus, broccoli, cauliflower, or Italian green beans.

2 pounds asparagus spears or other vegetable as suggested above
3 egg yolks
½ cup dry white wine
½ teaspoon salt
1 teaspoon lemon juice
½ teaspoon Dijon-style mustard
several turns freshly ground white pepper (optional)

Peel the ends of the asparagus using a vegetable peeler. Cook in a small amount of boiling salted water or steam until tender; drain and turn into a serving bowl. Place in the top of a double boiler the egg yolks, wine, salt, lemon juice, mustard, and pepper. Beat with a wire whisk until blended and cook over simmering water, whisking constantly, until sauce doubles in volume and thickens. Spoon over vegetable and serve at once. Serves 8. Contains about 40 calories per serving.

Cold Artichokes Piquant

Spicy Mexican seasonings — cilantro, cumin, orégano, garlic, and red peppers — flatter cold boiled artichokes.

6 large artichokes
boiling salted water seasoned with ¼ cup lemon juice and 1 tablespoon salad oil
2 tablespoons each sesame oil and white-wine vinegar
1 tablespoon each olive oil and lemon juice
1 tablespoon finely chopped cilantro
1 shallot or green onion, finely chopped
½ teaspoon Mexican seasoning (a blend of cumin, orégano, garlic, and red peppers)

Using a sharp knife, cut off the stem of the artichokes to make a flat base. Pull off the outer leaves and then, with scissors, cut off the thorns on the remaining leaves. Cook in a large kettle in about 4 quarts of boiling salted seasoned water, allowing 40 to 50 minutes for the large artichokes. Drain and chill.

Mix together a dressing composed of the sesame oil, vinegar, olive oil, lemon juice, cilantro, shallot, and Mexican seasoning. Cover and chill. Serve each person a whole artichoke on a plate with the dressing poured into a small dish alongside, or poured into the depression of artichoke plates. Serves 6. Contains about 115 calories per serving.

Artichokes Athena

The Greek way with "thistles" results in lovely fresh-colored little chokes, aromatic with herbs.

2½ pounds baby artichokes
water bath: see below
7 tablespoons lemon juice
salt
paprika
3 tablespoons minced parsley
1 teaspoon crumbled dried orégano
1 tablespoon olive oil

Peel artichokes way down, discarding the tough leaves; halve and scoop out choke. Drop into the Water Bath (see below). Bring 2 quarts water to boil in a large kettle, add 3 tablespoons of lemon juice, salt to taste, and drained artichokes. Cover and simmer 15 to 20 minutes, or until tender. Drain. Turn into a serving bowl. Sprinkle with paprika, parsley, orégano, and remaining lemon juice and oil. Makes 6 servings. Contains about 65 calories per serving.

Water Bath: Half fill a large bowl with water and add ¼ cup flour, ⅓ cup lemon juice, and 2 teaspoons salt. The combination of flour and lemon juice prevents the artichokes from darkening.

Carrots Orangerie

Orange marmalade glamorizes the humble carrot with a tangy sweet glaze.

1½ pounds carrots (about 6 medium-sized ones)
boiling salted water
1½ tablespoons orange marmalade
1 tablespoon butter or margarine
dash nutmeg

Peel carrots and slice thinly on the diagonal. Cook in a large, covered frying pan in a small amount of boiling salted water until almost tender; drain. Add marmalade, butter, and nutmeg and heat, stirring occasionally, until carrots are glazed. Makes 6 servings. Contains about 65 calories per ¾-cup serving.

Carrots Normandy Style

Cooked apple lends an intriguing tart sweetness to this smooth carrot purée.

6 large carrots
1 large tart apple
salt and pepper to taste
dash freshly ground nutmeg
2 tablespoons rich chicken broth

Peel carrots and cut in 1-inch pieces. Peel, core, and slice apple. Place carrots and apple in a saucepan, add ¼-inch water, and season with salt and pepper. Cover and simmer until tender, about 15 minutes. Drain. Place in a blender or food processor, add nutmeg and chicken broth, and blend until smooth. Serve hot. Makes 4 servings. Contains 50 calories per serving.

Cauliflower Orégano

Lemon juice and herbs transform snow-white cauliflowerets.

1 large head cauliflower
2 tablespoons lemon juice
¾ teaspoon crumbled dried orégano
1 clove garlic, minced
¼ teaspoon salt
1 tablespoon minced parsley

Separate cauliflower into flowerets and cook in boiling salted water until barely tender; drain. Place in a serving bowl. Mix together the lemon juice, orégano, garlic, salt, and parsley and spoon over the cauliflower. Makes 6 servings. Contains about 23 calories per ¾-cup serving.

Artichoke Variation: If desired, cook cauliflower whole, in boiling salted water; drain. Place on a platter and surround with 2 packages (9 ounces each) frozen artichoke hearts, parboiled just until tender. Double the recipe for the lemon dressing and spoon over the cauliflower and artichokes.

Crookneck with Herbs

Simmered in chicken stock and herbs, golden crookneck squash attains superb flavor.

4 small yellow crookneck squash (about 1 pound)
2 tablespoons rich concentrated chicken stock
½ teaspoon crumbled dried basil
¼ teaspoon each onion powder and garlic salt
freshly ground pepper

Trim ends from squash and cut in half lengthwise. Place squash in a saucepan with stock, basil, onion powder, garlic salt, and pepper. Cover and simmer 7 to 8 minutes, or until vegetables are crisp tender. Makes 4 servings. Contains about 20 calories per serving.

Green Beans Italian

A fresh vegetable dressing cloaks french-cut green beans.

1 ½ pounds green beans
1 tablespoon minced shallots or green onions
1 clove garlic
1 teaspoon whipped margarine
2 tomatoes, peeled and chopped
1 ounce proscuitto or ham, diced
2 tablespoons chopped parsley

Trim ends from green beans and french-cut. Cook beans in boiling salted water until crisp tender; drain. Sauté shallots and garlic in margarine until just glazed. Add tomatoes and proscuitto and mix lightly. Mix in beans. Turn into a serving bowl and sprinkle with parsley. Makes 6 servings. Contains 45 calories per serving.

Green Bean Strata

Double layers of a cottage cheese custard enhance the humble bean.

1 ½ pounds green beans
2 tablespoons minced onion
salt and pepper to taste
½ teaspoon crushed dried tarragon
3 eggs
¾ cup small-curd cottage cheese
3 tablespoons each chopped parsley and chopped green onion
½ cup grated Swiss cheese

Trim ends from beans and cut into julienne strips. Cook in boiling salted water with onion, salt, pepper, and tarragon until crisp tender; drain. Beat eggs and mix in cottage cheese, parsley, onions, and all but 2 tablespoons Swiss cheese. Alternate beans and cheese mixture in a buttered baking dish, ending with cheese mixture. Sprinkle remaining cheese on top. Bake in a 350° oven for 25 minutes or until cheese is melted and topping is set. Serves 6. Contains 120 calories per serving.

Indian Eggplant Slices

A brilliant trio of vegetables offers a tantalizing counterpoint of
flavors, colors, and temperatures.

1 large eggplant, sliced ¾-inch thick
salt
1 medium-sized onion, chopped
1 teaspoon salad or olive oil
⅓ cup tomato paste
3 medium-sized tomatoes, peeled and chopped
1 teaspoon finely chopped fresh ginger root
½ teaspoon salt
6 tablespoons low-fat yogurt

Sprinkle eggplant slices with salt and let them stand to remove excess
moisture. Sauté onion in oil until golden. Add tomato paste,
tomatoes, ginger root, and salt; cover and simmer 30 minutes or until
very tender. Meanwhile, rinse off the eggplant slices and arrange on a
lightly greased baking pan. Bake in a 425° oven for 25 minutes or
until tender. Arrange eggplant on a platter, spoon the tomato sauce
over it, and top each slice with a spoonful of yogurt. Serves 6.
Contains about 75 calories per serving.

Ratatouille

The abundance from the garden or marketplace makes a beautiful vegetable potpourri to accompany broiled skewered shrimp or lamb nuggets.

1 small eggplant
salt
4 green onions, chopped
4 small zucchini, thinly sliced
3 cloves garlic, minced
1 small red or green pepper, diced, with seeds removed
2 teaspoons olive oil
2 tomatoes, peeled and chopped
1 teaspoon each salt and fresh chopped basil
2 tablespoons chopped parsley

Quarter eggplant, sprinkle with salt, and let stand 15 minutes. Then rinse off and pat dry with paper towels. Dice into bite-sized pieces. Using a dutch oven or flameproof casserole, sauté onions, zucchini, garlic, and pepper in oil a few minutes, stirring. Add eggplant, tomatoes, salt, and basil. Cover and simmer 10 minutes. Remove cover and let boil until juices are reduced and thickened. Sprinkle with parsley. Good hot or cold. Makes 4 servings. Contains about 50 calories per serving.

Green Pea and Spinach Soufflé

This grass-green soufflé complements broiled fish kebabs, poached chicken, or beef or lamb roast.

1 package (10 ounces) frozen petit peas, cooked
¾ cup yogurt
2 tablespoons chopped shallots
1 cup chopped fresh spinach leaves
½ tablespoon crumbled dried marjoram
2 tablespoons parsley
2 eggs, separated
4 egg whites
1 teaspoon salt
2 tablespoons cornstarch
1 tablespoon grated Parmesan cheese

Purée peas in a blender with yogurt, shallots, spinach, marjoram, parsley, and egg yolks. Beat the 6 egg whites until foamy, add salt and cornstarch and beat until stiff. Fold in pea purée. Turn into a greased 1½-quart soufflé dish. Sprinkle with cheese. Bake in a 325° oven for 30 to 35 minutes or until set. Makes 8 servings. Contains about 100 calories per serving.

Ricotta Chile Pepper Soufflé

This peppery, light soufflé is lovely with a fresh fruit plate for a
Mexican-style brunch.

4 eggs, separated
½ teaspoon salt
1 tablespoon cornstarch
¼ teaspoon dry mustard
dash Tabasco
¾ cup sour half-and-half
¾ cup ricotta or dry cottage cheese
1 can (4 ounces) diced chile peppers
2 egg whites

Beat egg yolks until thick and pale in color and beat in salt,
cornstarch, mustard, and Tabasco. Mix in sour half-and-half, ricotta,
and chile peppers. Beat the 6 egg whites until stiff, but not dry, and
fold in. Turn into a greased 1½-quart soufflé dish. Place in a pan of
hot water and bake in a 325° oven for 1 hour. Serves 6. Contains
160 calories per serving.

Sherry Sautéed Mushrooms

Give mushrooms a quick "flash in the pan" so they retain their
ambrosial juices. Then spoon them over vegetable soufflés, sliced
beef or veal roasts, or baked chicken breasts.

1 pound mushrooms
2 tablespoons chopped shallots
1 tablespoon whipped margarine
3 tablespoons pale dry Sherry
2 tablespoons minced parsley

Wash and slice mushrooms. Using a large frying pan, sauté shallots
in margarine until glazed. Add mushrooms and sauté quickly. Add
Sherry and cook down until juices are slightly reduced. Sprinkle with
parsley. Makes 4 to 6 servings. Contains 32 to 50 calories per
serving.

Italian Spinach Pie

This stunning vegetable *torta,* in the Italian vernacular, is superb warm or cold. It goes with salami and cheeses on a picnic or enhances a roast for a party dinner.

Italian egg pastry: see below
2 medium-sized onions, chopped
1 bunch green onions, chopped
2 teaspoons olive oil
3 bunches spinach, washed and chopped, or 2 spinach and 1 Swiss chard (about 3 pounds greens)
3 cloves garlic, minced
8 ounces ricotta cheese
5 eggs, lightly beaten
2 teaspoons salt
½ teaspoon each crumbled dried tarragon and freshly ground pepper
1 cup shredded Romano or Parmesan cheese

First prepare Italian Egg Pastry: see below. Roll out to a 16-inch circle and place in a 10-inch cheesecake or springform pan (with removable bottom), letting the dough cover bottom and sides of pan and drape over the outsides about 1½ inches. Sauté onions in oil until limp. Add spinach and garlic and cook until wilted; press out any extra liquid. Turn into a bowl and mix in ricotta, eggs, salt, tarragon, pepper, and ¾ cup of the Romano cheese. Turn into the pastry-lined pan and fold the overlapping dough back over the tart. Sprinkle the spinach filling that shows with remaining Romano. Bake in a 425° oven for 15 minutes; reduce heat to 375° and bake 15 minutes longer, or until set. Let cool slightly before serving. Makes 12 servings. Contains 120 calories per serving.

Italian Egg Pastry: Sprinkle 1 teaspoon yeast into 1 tablespoon water in a mixing bowl. Let stand until dissolved. Add 1 egg, ¼ teaspoon salt, and 1 teaspoon olive oil and beat until blended. Add ⅓ cup each all-purpose flour and whole wheat flour and beat until smooth. Knead on a floured board 1 or 2 minutes to shape into a ball. Cover with plastic wrap and let stand 20 minutes before rolling.

Spinach and Mushroom Filo Roll

Filo dough encases a fat roll of chopped spinach and mushrooms for a savory, golden-brown pastry.

1 large onion, finely chopped
1 bunch green onions, chopped
2 tablespoons melted butter
¼ pound mushrooms, chopped
1½ pounds spinach, finely chopped
¼ cup chopped parsley
⅛ teaspoon nutmeg
salt and pepper to taste
3 eggs, beaten
¼ cup each shredded Parmesan and Swiss cheese
5 sheets filo dough

Using a large frying pan, sauté onion and green onions in 1 teaspoon butter until limp. Add mushrooms and cook until glazed. Add spinach and heat until barely wilted. Remove from heat and drain off any extra liquid. Mix in parsley, nutmeg, salt, pepper, eggs, and cheese. Lay out 1 sheet of filo and brush lightly with melted butter; cover with a second sheet, butter lightly, and repeat layering remaining sheets and buttering between. Spoon spinach mixture along a long side; fold up ends of filo 1 inch and roll up the dough, encasing the spinach. Place seam side down on a lightly buttered pan. Bake in 375° oven for 40 minutes or until crispy and browned. Cut in 2-inch slices and serve warm. Makes 6 servings. Contains about 100 calories per serving.

Spinach Ricotta Balls

Italian spinach dumplings are an excellent party entrée. Plan to make them in advance as they reheat very well.

1 package (10 ounces) frozen chopped spinach, thawed and squeezed dry
½ pint ricotta cheese
1 egg, lightly beaten
¼ teaspoon salt
1 green onion, finely minced
2 tablespoons chopped parsley
½ cup freshly shredded Parmesan cheese
3 tablespoons fine dry bread crumbs
whole-wheat flour
1½ quarts water

Mix together in a large bowl the spinach, ricotta, egg, salt, onion, parsley, 6 tablespoons cheese, and bread crumbs. Shape into walnut-sized balls and roll lightly in flour. Bring water to a boil, add a few balls at a time, and let simmer 5 minutes, or until balls float to the top. Lift out to a heat-proof serving platter and continue to cook remaining balls. Sprinkle with remaining cheese. Slip under the broiler to brown lightly. Makes 4 servings. Contains about 200 calories per serving.

Spinach Frittata

Cartwheels of tomato brighten this neat spinach "pie."

1 bunch fresh spinach, stems removed
1 bunch green onions, chopped
¼ cup nonfat dry milk solids
½ cup water
2 eggs
½ teaspoon salt
¼ teaspoon dried tarragon
¼ cup shredded Parmesan cheese
1 large tomato, thinly sliced
low-fat yogurt

Place washed spinach and onions in a large frying pan over medium-high heat and cook 1 minute, uncovered, until barely limp. Turn into a blender container and add milk solids, water, eggs, salt, tarragon, and half the cheese. Blend until finely minced. Turn into a lightly buttered 9-inch pie pan and arrange tomato slices on top. Sprinkle with remaining cheese and bake in a 350° oven for 30 minutes or until set. Cut in wedges and serve with a spoonful of yogurt. Makes 6 servings. Contains 65 calories per serving.

Spinach-Stuffed Zucchini

Feta cheese and spinach fill squash half shells for a refined vegetable dish.

4 medium-sized zucchini (about 1¼ pounds)
1 bunch spinach (about 1 pound)
1 egg
½ cup crumbled feta cheese (about 2 ounces)
dash each garlic salt, freshly ground pepper, and ground nutmeg
½ cup shredded Parmesan cheese

Trim ends from zucchini, halve lengthwise, and cook in boiling salted water for 5 minutes; drain, reserving liquid. Hollow out the insides slightly and discard pulp. Wash and chop spinach and cook until limp; drain thoroughly and chop again until finely minced. Then pat dry. Beat egg and mix in feta, garlic salt, pepper, nutmeg, and spinach. Pile into the squash half shells and sprinkle with cheese. Lay on a baking pan and pour in reserved liquid from squash. If desired, cover with foil and refrigerate until serving time. Bake covered in a 350° oven for 20 minutes, then remove foil and bake 10 minutes longer or until top is lightly browned (reduce baking time 10 to 15 minutes if not chilled). Makes 8 servings. Contains 70 calories per serving.

Spinach Soufflé

Fresh spinach colors this soufflé a bright grassy green.

1 bunch spinach, stems removed
4 eggs, separated
2 green onions, chopped
¼ cup chopped parsley
2 tablespoons cornstarch
¼ cup nonfat dry milk solids
¾ cup water
½ teaspoon salt
¼ teaspoon freshly ground pepper
¼ cup shredded Parmesan or Romano cheese

Rinse spinach leaves, then place in a large frying pan and cook uncovered with just the water clinging to the leaves barely 1 minute, or until just heated. Turn into the blender container and blend with egg yolks until puréed. Mix in onions and parsley. Combine cornstarch, milk solids, and water in a saucepan and cook until thickened. Season with salt and pepper. Stir in spinach purée. Beat egg whites until stiff but not dry and fold in. Mix in 2 tablespoons cheese. Turn into a buttered baking dish, such as a 10-inch round casserole or 1½-quart soufflé dish. Sprinkle remaining cheese on top. Bake in a 350° oven for 30 minutes or until puffed and lightly browned on top. Serves 6. Contains 100 calories per serving.

Shredded Zucchini

When squash from the garden becomes a bit oversized, this is a fine way to cook it as the extra moisture is squeezed out first.

2 pounds zucchini
2 green onions, chopped
¼ cup chopped parsley
½ teaspoon garlic salt
freshly ground pepper

Trim ends from squash and shred it finely. Turn it into a tea towel and squeeze out the extra moisture. Turn into a large frying pan. Season with onions, parsley, garlic salt, and pepper. Cover and simmer 2 minutes, then remove cover and cook down any juices over medium-high heat. Makes 4 to 6 servings. Contains 20 to 25 calories per ¾-cup serving.

Zucchini Orégano

The fresh sparkle of herbs and onion enhances this crisp-tender squash dish.

2 pounds zucchini, sliced
1 medium-sized onion, chopped
2 cloves garlic, minced
½ teaspoon crumbled dried orégano
1 tablespoon tomato paste
salt and pepper to taste
1 tablespoon olive oil

Place in a saucepan the zucchini, onion, garlic, orégano, tomato paste, salt, pepper, and oil; cover and steam 6 to 8 minutes or until crisp tender. Makes 6 servings. Contains about 40 calories per serving.

Fruit Desserts

It is hard to surpass the pleasures offered by a bowl of sun-kissed raspberries, a wedge of vine-ripened crenshaw, or spears of a drippingly juicy Comice pear. The fruits alone are superb, but sometimes they are made even more delicious by a splash of liqueur or a bath of wine. Here we explore the compatible mating of melon sparked with the spice of cilantro, pineapple paired with the crunch of praline, and strawberries laced with Cointreau.

Flowers from the garden add charm to the presentation of fruit. Fuschias are pretty tucked in berry bowls. Cyclamen brighten winter fruit trays. Nasturtiums add color to a melon basket, and a wreath of marguerites lends whimsy to a platter of lemon shells holding fruit ices.

The following fruit combinations may be swiftly assembled and chilled in advance.

Watermelon-Grape Bowl

Mingle chilled spears of watermelon and Thompson seedless grapes in large-bowled wine glasses.

Strawberry-Raspberry Bowl

Combine 3 cups halved strawberries and 1 cup raspberries in a bowl. Sprinkle with 2 teaspoons sugar and drizzle with 1 tablespoon kirsch or framboise. Chill and serve in dessert bowls.

Pineapple Spears in Rum

Marinate spears of fresh pineapple in a light dousing of rum or kirsch. Serve on dessert plates.

Peaches with Galliano

Peel and slice fresh Babcock peaches or other white peaches. Spoon into dessert bowls and sprinkle with Galliano liqueur.

Berries on Ice

Serve long-stemmed strawberries on a bed of crushed ice.

Zig-Zag Melon Boats

Slice crenshaw or honeydew melon into wedges, remove seeds, and with a grapefruit knife cut fruit free from the skin. Cut melon into ½-inch thick slices and return to the shell, arranging slices in a zig-zag pattern. Garnish with a wedge of lime and a blossom.

Peaches Melba Style

Peel and halve peaches and arrange in dessert bowls. Pour puréed raspberries over them and garnish with a dollop of yogurt.

Melon Baskets

Cut small cantaloupes in half, scoop out seeds, and make balls with a melon-ball cutter. Scoop out remaining fruit making a neat shell. Combine the cantaloupe balls with an equal amount of watermelon and honeydew melon balls, drizzle with Cointreau or other orange-flavored liqueur, and spoon into the melon half shells. Garnish each with a sprig of mint.

Cantaloupe Halves with Berries

Halve small cantaloupe using a zig-zag cut design and scoop out the seeds. Fill the center cavities with strawberries and drizzle with a little kirsch.

Honeydew Surprise

Cut 4 wedges from a whole honeydew melon, leaving the rest of the melon attached, and scoop out seeds. Arrange on a platter with each wedge pointing outward from where it was cut from the melon. Fill the inner shell of the melon with watermelon balls or strawberries.

Blossoms and Iced Fruit

Float fresh fruit, such as light or dark cherries, apricots, plums, or nectarines, and a flower blossom or two in a crystal bowl filled with cold water and ice cubes, as the Italians do.

Yogurt Avocado Sherbet

Garnish this pale green sherbet with a few strawberries, diced papaya, or pineapple, if you wish.

1 large avocado
1 cup low-fat yogurt
⅓ cup honey
3 tablespoons lime or lemon juice
dash salt
2 egg whites

Halve avocado, remove seed, and scoop out fruit, placing it in a blender container. Add yogurt, honey, lime juice, and salt. Beat egg whites until soft peaks form and fold into the avocado mixture. Turn into fluted molds and freeze until firm. Dip into hot water to unmold. Makes 6 servings. Contains 120 calories per serving.

Apricots and Cheese Pyramid

This liqueur-scented cheese spread is suave on other fresh fruits such as halved nectarines or sliced apples or pears.

1 cup (8 ounces) ricotta cheese
¼ cup powdered sugar
2 tablespoons Cointreau or other orange-flavored liqueur
16 fresh apricots (approximately)

Beat together the cheese, sugar, and Cointreau and mound in a serving bowl. Chill. When ready to serve, surround with halved apricots. Spread the cheese on each apricot half. Makes 8 servings. Contains about 120 calories per serving.

Bananas Flambé

The festivity of flambéing lends drama to a meal.

1 tablespoon butter
2 tablespoons sugar
¼ cup orange-juice concentrate, thawed (undiluted)
4 bananas
2 tablespoons rum
grated chocolate curls

Melt butter in a chafing dish or frying pan. Add sugar and orange concentrate and bring to a boil. Peel and slice bananas on the diagonal. Arrange in the pan and flame with rum. Spoon onto dessert plates and garnish with chocolate curls. Makes 4 servings. Contains about 180 calories per serving.

Crenshaw with Coriander

The spiciness of fresh cilantro uplifts lime-dressed melon.

1 small crenshaw melon
¼ cup lime juice
1½ tablespoons honey
1 tablespoon finely chopped cilantro

Peel melon, halve, remove seeds, and cut into spears. Mix together the lime juice, honey, and cilantro and spoon over the melon. Cover and chill 1 hour. Serve in dessert bowls. Makes 6 to 8 servings. Contains about 30 to 40 calories per serving.

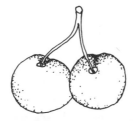

Ruby Fruit Bowl

The zest of citrus peels marries with the ruby berry juices to scent this fruit bowl.

1 each orange, lemon, and lime
⅓ cup sugar
2 cups watermelon balls
2 cups strawberries
2 cups seedless grapes

Grate the peel from the citrus fruits and set aside. Halve fruit and squeeze out juice. Place in a saucepan with sugar and heat just until sugar is dissolved. Let cool; add fruit peel. Place in a bowl the melon balls, berries, and grapes and pour over citrus syrup. Chill. Makes 6 to 8 servings. Contains about 100 to 125 calories per serving.

Fruit Ice

A frosty fruit purée makes an appealing ice, especially when mounded in a melon ring or shell.

3 cups honeydew, crenshaw, or watermelon purée
¼ cup sugar
3 tablespoons lime juice

Combine the puréed fruit with sugar and lime juice and pour into a shallow pan. Freeze until solid. Pour into a mixing bowl and chop up with a wooden spoon. Beat slowly with an electric mixer, then more rapidly until smooth and thick. Return to pan and refreeze. Spoon onto complementary wedges or rings of melon. Some good combinations are: watermelon ice with honeydew crescents; honeydew ice with watermelon balls; crenshaw ice inside small cantaloupe halves. Makes about 3 cups, or 4 to 6 servings. Contains about 50 to 70 calories per serving.

Strawberry or Pineapple Ice: Follow the directions above except omit lime juice. Serve strawberry ice with raspberries, and pineapple ice with strawberries.

Chilled Mandarin Soufflé

This airy light dessert is wonderfully refreshing after fish, chicken, or veal.

1 envelope unflavored gelatin
1 cup orange juice
1 tablespoon lemon juice
½ teaspoon grated orange peel
3 egg whites
¼ cup sugar
1 can (11 ounces) mandarin oranges

Sprinkle gelatin over orange juice and let stand until softened. Dissolve over hot water. Stir in lemon juice and orange peel. Let chill until syrupy. Beat egg whites until soft peaks form and beat in sugar. Fold in gelatin mixture. Spoon into dessert bowls and garnish with oranges. Chill until set. Makes 6 servings. Contains about 75 calories per serving.

Oranges Moroccan

From the palette of orange, red, and green tones comes this striking fruit plate.

2 large navel oranges, peeled and thinly sliced
1 cup strawberries, hulled
1 tablespoon Cointreau or other orange-flavored liqueur
1 tablespoon pistachio nuts, coarsely chopped

Peel a thin strip of orange zest from the orange peel and cut into thin slivers. Arrange orange slices on dessert plates in an overlapping pattern and cluster halved or whole strawberries in the center. Toss the finely cut zest with the liqueur and spoon over the berries. Sprinkle with nuts. Makes 4 servings. Contains about 65 calories per serving.

Caramelized Oranges

A burnt-sugar syrup offers a rewarding sauce on fresh sliced juicy oranges. Each fruit is peeled, then reassembled in its original shape for a decorative look.

½ cup sugar
¼ cup hot water
¼ cup orange juice
6 large seedless oranges

Pour sugar into a heavy frying pan and place over moderately high heat until it dissolves and caramelizes. Carefully pour in the hot water and orange juice and heat until smoothly blended, shaking the pan. Let cool. With a vegetable peeler, peel off the zest of the orange and simmer in boiling water a few minutes; drain and cut into slivers. Cut the rind, pith, and first membrane from the oranges and thinly slice. Reassemble into an orange shape and skewer with a toothpick. Arrange on a serving dish, pour over the caramel, and sprinkle with the julienne orange strips. Chill thoroughly. Makes 6 servings. Contains about 150 calories per serving.

Snow Peaches with Raspberry Sauce

The brilliance of raspberry purée on pale white summer peaches makes a magnificent dessert.

4 white Babcock peaches
1 package (10 ounces) frozen raspberries, thawed

Purée raspberries in a blender and push through a wire strainer to remove seeds. Peel and slice peaches and place in dessert bowls. Pour over berry purée. Makes 4 servings. Contains 90 calories per serving.

Papaya and Blueberry Boats

This striking fruit pair — from the tropics and the mountains — might precede a brunch or conclude a dinner featuring poultry or fish.

2 small papayas
1½ cups blueberries
1 tablespoon powdered sugar
lime wedges

Halve papayas and remove seeds. Fill cavities with berries and dust lightly with powdered sugar. Serve on dessert plates with lime wedges. Makes 4 servings. Contains 40 calories per serving.

Note: Another suggestion is to serve peeled slices of papaya with finely chopped crystallized ginger and lime wedges.

Papaya Fruit Plate

An ornamental arrangement of brilliant fruits makes an enticing climax to dinner.

1 papaya
1 kiwi
1 cup large strawberries
1 lime

Peel, halve, and seed papaya and cut into strips. Peel and thinly slice kiwi. Arrange on 4 dessert plates a few slices of papaya overlapped with a slice or two of kiwi. Place berries in a cluster and garnish with lime wedges. Serves 4. Contains about 50 calories per serving.

Papaya Honey Sherbet

This is an exotic way to finish a summer salad luncheon or barbecue dinner.

1 large ripe papaya
1 cup orange juice
2 tablespoons lime or lemon juice
¼ cup honey
2 egg whites
1 lime, cut in wedges

Peel and halve papaya and scoop out seeds; dice fruit. Put in a blender container with orange juice, lime juice, and honey. Purée until smooth. Pour into a freezer container and freeze until just solid. Remove from the freezer and turn into a mixing bowl. Beat with an electric mixer, starting at low and gradually increasing to high speed, until smooth and slushy. Beat egg whites until soft peaks form, and fold into the papaya mixture. Turn into a freezer container, cover, and freeze until firm. Serve in dessert bowls or wine glasses and garnish with a lime wedge. Makes about 1 quart. Makes 6 servings. Contains about 80 calories per serving.

Persimmons with Lime

During their brief December season, the striking beauty of orange persimmons with lime is a tantalizing finale. Simply slice the stem end from a ripe persimmon and squeeze over it a light drizzle of lime juice. Eat with a spoon, out of the shell, in a dessert bowl. For out of season, freeze the whole fruit, sealed in a plastic bag. Peel and slice while still frosty and squeeze lime juice over it. Contains 75 calories for 1 persimmon.

Pears in Variation

Throughout the year we can enjoy a succession of pear desserts, thanks to the juicy winter Comice or Anjou varieties, followed by the summer Bartlett. Any is superb when cut into spears and garnished discreetly. For ease, use an apple corer to slice through a whole pear in one motion, at once removing the core and cutting the fruit into spears. Place in a dessert bowl, points up. Sprinkle over each serving 1 teaspoon Cointreau, Chartreuse, or framboise liqueurs. Or sprinkle over each 1 teaspoon finely chopped crystallized ginger. Or purée 1 package (12 ounces) frozen raspberries and press through a wire strainer, discarding seeds. Spoon about 2 tablespoons raspberry purée over each serving. Allow about 75 calories for the pear, 10 for each liqueur, and 25 for the ginger or berry purée.

Pineapple Alaska

A golden mask of meringue seals sherbet inside hollowed-out pineapple shells.

1 medium-sized pineapple
1 pint lemon or lime sherbet or ice
3 egg whites
dash each salt and cream of tartar
⅓ cup sugar

Wash pineapple but do not remove leaves. With a sharp knife, cut pineapple in half lengthwise, cutting through the leaves. Using a grapefruit knife, cut out the pineapple and remove from shell. Dice fruit, discarding the core. Spoon half the fruit back into the shells. Spoon mounds of sherbet on top and cover with remaining pineapple. Cover with plastic wrap and place in the freezer until sherbet is firm again. Beat egg whites until foamy, add salt and cream of tartar, and beat until soft peaks form. Gradually beat in sugar, beating until stiff. Spread meringue over pineapple. Place in a 450° oven for 5 minutes or just until meringue browns. Arrange on a platter and bring to the table to serve.
Makes 6 servings. Contains about 150 calories per serving.

Pineapple Boats

This decorative way of cutting fresh pineapple works well on melon wedges also.

**1 small to medium-sized pineapple
1½ cups fresh strawberries
1 lime, cut in wedges**

Cut pineapple into quarters, lengthwise, leaving plume intact. With a grapefruit knife cut between the peel and fruit and slice underneath the core. Remove the fruit section and cut crosswise into ¾-inch slices. Return to shell poking every other slice in about ½ inch and place berries in the opening. Garnish with lime. Makes 4 servings. Contains about 120 calories per serving.

Pineapple Soufflé

A hot pineapple soufflé makes an ethereal dessert after almost any entrée.

**1¼ cups canned crushed pineapple (water pack)
6 tablespoons sugar
2 tablespoons each cornstarch and cold water
4 eggs, separated
1 teaspoon vanilla
½ teaspoon salt
2 egg whites**

Drain liquid from pineapple and measure; you should have ¾ cup. Bring to a boil with ¼ cup sugar and stir in a paste of cornstarch and water. Cook, stirring, until thickened. Mix in egg yolks, vanilla, and salt. Beat the 6 egg whites until soft peaks form and beat in remaining 2 tablespoons sugar. Fold in the pineapple mixture. Turn into a buttered 2-quart soufflé dish. Bake in a 375° oven for 30 to 35 minutes or until set. Makes 6 servings. Contains 110 calories per serving.

Pineapple Buttermilk Sherbet

If you like, freeze this sherbet in hollowed-out orange or lemon shells.

2 cups buttermilk
½ cup sugar
1 teaspoon grated lemon peel
1 cup crushed pineapple
1 slightly beaten egg white
1 teaspoon vanilla
mint sprigs

Combine buttermilk, sugar, lemon peel, and pineapple and let stand until sugar dissolves. Pour into a freezer container and freeze until barely firm. Turn into a chilled bowl, add egg white and vanilla, and beat until light and fluffy. Return to a freezer container and freeze until firm. Makes 6 servings. Contains about 120 calories per serving.

Pineapple and Praline Diamonds

The brittle snap of praline is a delightful contrast to juice-laden pineapple sticks.

1 medium-sized pineapple
2 tablespoons rum or kirsch (optional)
6 tablespoons sugar
¼ cup sliced almonds

Peel pineapple and slice lengthwise into ¾-inch wide sticks, discarding core. Let marinate in liqueur, if desired. Heat sugar in a small frying pan over medium-high heat until it turns liquid and amber in color. Add nuts and shake until coated. Turn out at once onto a sheet of buttered foil. With a buttered spatula, spread into a thin layer. While still warm, cut into diamond-shaped pieces. Let cool. Place 3 sticks of pineapple on a plate or in a goblet or wine glass and garnish with a praline diamond. Makes 4 servings. Contains about 120 calories per serving.

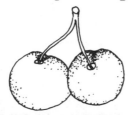

Zabaglione with Raspberries

The frothy Italian wine custard is a beautiful match for raspberries.

6 egg yolks
6 tablespoons sugar
½ cup dry white wine, such as Chablis Blanc
1 teaspoon grated lemon peel
2 cups raspberries or strawberries

In the top of a double boiler, beat egg yolks until light and beat in sugar, wine, and lemon peel. Place over simmering water and beat with a wire whip or portable electric beater until it triples in volume and retains a peak, about 7 minutes. Cool immediately by placing pan in a pan of ice water; then chill. Using tall, slender glasses, alternate spoonfuls of zabaglione and berries. Serves 6. Contains about 125 calories per serving.

Hot Variation: Spoon 1 tablespoon grenadine in each glass and pour in hot zabaglione. Omit berries. Serve at once.

Strawberries Laced with Pistachios and Cointreau

Chopped green pistachios lend contrast to scarlet berries.

2 cups ripe strawberries
2 tablespoons Cointreau
1 tablespoon powdered sugar
2 tablespoons chopped pistachios

Wash, hull, and halve berries. Place in a bowl and toss with Cointreau and sugar. Let stand 15 minutes. Serve in dessert bowls and sprinkle with nuts. Makes 4 servings. Contains about 55 calories per serving.

Strawberries in Wine

One of the most effective French desserts, and a simple one, is berries steeped in wine. Serve in champagne or large-bowled burgundy glasses so you can savor the fruit-kissed wine at the end.

3 cups strawberries
¼ cup sugar
1½ cups dry red wine, such as Zinfandel or a red Bordeaux

Wash and hull berries. Alternate layers of berries and sugar in a wide-mouthed, tall cylindrical jar or glass serving container. Pour over enough wine to cover. Let stand at room temperature at least 4 hours. Serves 4. Contains about 180 calories per serving.

Wine Sabayon with Strawberries

A delicate, hot, frothy wine custard gilds cool, juicy strawberries.

6 egg yolks
¼ cup sugar
⅔ cup dry white wine
½ teaspoon grated lemon peel
2 tablespoons kirsch or brandy
3 cups strawberries, washed and hulled

In the top of a double boiler beat egg yolks and sugar until blended. Beat in wine. Beat over simmering water using a wire whisk or an electric beater until sauce is thick and custard-like. Remove from heat and stir in kirsch. Spoon berries into dessert bowls and pour the wine custard over them. Makes 6 servings. Contains about 150 calories per serving.

Strawberries in Champagne

Berries scent Champagne sweetly as you sip it; afterwards savor the wine-steeped fruit.

2 cups strawberries
small bottle Champagne

Wash, hull, and slice berries and spoon into 7-ounce wine or Champagne glasses. Pour in Champagne. Serve at once. Serves 4. Contains about 100 calories per serving.

Raspberry Yogurt Parfait

Raspberries marbleize this delicate yogurt mousse, sparked with orange.

1 egg white
3 tablespoons dark brown sugar, firmly packed
1 cup low-fat plain or vanilla-flavored yogurt
1 tablespoon frozen orange-juice concentrate, thawed, or orange liqueur
2 cups fresh raspberries or halved strawberries

Beat egg white until soft peaks form. Add sugar and beat until stiff. Fold in yogurt and orange-juice concentrate. Alternate spoonfuls of yogurt mousse and berries in parfait glasses or slender wine glasses. Makes 4 servings. Contains 100 calories per serving.

Summer Shimmer Tart

Here's a crustless fruit tart with a glistening festive look.

1 envelope unflavored gelatin
1½ cups orange juice
1 tablespoon lemon juice
1 tablespoon sugar
1 teaspoon each grated orange and lemon peel
4 nectarines
4 plums
1½ cups strawberries
1½ cups seedless grapes
1 small cantaloupe, cut in balls
Sour half-and-half
Raw or brown sugar

Select a large, 11-inch round platter to compose this dessert. Soften gelatin in cold orange juice. Heat over hot water until dissolved. Stir in lemon juice, sugar, and orange and lemon peel. Let cool slightly. Slice nectarines and plums and arrange a circle of slices around the outer edge creating a pinwheel effect. Pour over enough gelatin to hold fruit in place and chill. When set, arrange hulled strawberries in a design in the center by placing a whole berry in the center and surrounding with halved berries, cut side up. Scatter grapes and melon balls over all. Pour over remaining gelatin and chill until set. Cut in wedges to serve. Accompany with sour half-and-half and raw or brown sugar to sprinkle over it. Serves 8. Contains about 100 to 150 calories per serving, depending on toppings used.

Other Sweets

Chocolate mousse, cheesecake, nut tortes, and soufflés can be within bounds for those tallying calories. To satisfy the "sweet tooth" most everyone has, these aim to please without upsetting the calorie basket.

Lemon Soufflé

This ambrosial tart soufflé makes a grand finale to a fish or chicken dinner.

3 tablespoons nonfat dry milk solids
1½ tablespoons cornstarch
¾ cup cold water
3 tablespoons lemon juice
2 teaspoons grated lemon peel
4 eggs, separated
2 egg whites
⅛ teaspoon each salt and cream of tartar
⅓ cup sugar

Stir together in a saucepan the milk solids, cornstarch, and water. Bring to a boil and cook until thickened, stirring constantly. Remove from heat and stir in lemon juice and peel. Mix in egg yolks, one at a time. Beat the 6 egg whites until foamy, add salt and cream of tartar, and beat until stiff. Beat in sugar. Stir part of the whites into the lemon sauce to lighten it; then fold in remaining whites. Turn into a buttered 1-quart soufflé dish or baking pan. Bake in a 350° oven for 45 minutes, or until set. Makes 6 servings. Contains 110 calories per serving.

Lemon Ice in Shells

The shells of squeezed-out citrus fruits — lemons, limes, or oranges
— make bright containers for a cool fruit ice.

4 lemons, limes, or oranges
lemon, lime, or orange ice or sherbet
citrus leaves or other garden leaves
orange-flavored liqueur (optional)

Slice off a thin lid from each fruit and cut a thin slice from the base so
it will stand upright. Use a grapefruit knife to scoop out the fruit and
use for marmalade or another purpose. Pack with fruit ice or sherbet.
Package airtight and freeze. To serve, place each fruit shell on a
dessert plate lined with a few leaves and spoon 1 teaspoon liqueur over
the ice, if desired. Place the lid on the shell. Makes 4 servings.
Contains about 140 calories per serving.

Basque Chocolate Mousse

Coffee and orange flavors blend with chocolate in this light mousse.

4 ounces semi-sweet chocolate bits
3 tablespoons coffee
1 tablespoon Cointreau or other orange-flavored liqueur
4 eggs, separated
1 teaspoon vanilla
1 tablespoon sugar

Place chocolate bits and coffee in a small metal bowl and heat in a
300° oven for 10 minutes, or until melted. Remove from oven and stir
in liqueur. Mix in egg yolks, one at a time. Stir in vanilla. Beat egg
whites until soft peaks form and add sugar, beating until stiff. Stir
one-third of the whites into the chocolate mixture. Fold in remaining
whites. Turn into 6 small dessert bowls. Cover and chill until set.
Makes 6 servings. Contains about 150 calories per serving.

Vanilla Bean Cheesecake

Yogurt and cottage cheese produce a remarkable cheesecake speckled with vanilla bean.

1 pint low-fat cottage cheese or ricotta cheese
½ pint low-fat yogurt
4 eggs
½ cup sugar
1½ teaspoons vanilla extract
1-inch piece vanilla bean, scraped

Place in a blender container the cottage cheese, yogurt, eggs, sugar, vanilla, and the scraped part of the vanilla bean. Blend just until smooth and pour into a lightly buttered 9-inch square pan. Place in a pan of hot water and bake in a 325° oven for 40 minutes or until set. Let cool and chill. Makes 12 to 16 servings. Contains 100 calories per 12-portion cheesecake, or 75 calories per 16-portion cheesecake.

Salzburger Nockerls

Assemble this Austrian puffy omelet just before baking.

4 eggs, separated
¼ cup sugar
¾ teaspoon grated lemon peel
1 tablespoon cornstarch
powdered sugar
2 tablespoons rum (optional)

Beat egg whites until soft peaks form and add sugar, beating until stiff. Beat yolks until thick and pale yellow in color and beat in lemon peel and cornstarch. Fold in the whites. Turn into a buttered 10-inch frying pan or baking dish. Bake in a 375° oven for 25 minutes or until golden brown. Dust with a thin film of powdered sugar. Warm rum, ignite, and spoon flaming over omelet. Makes 4 servings. Contains about 135 calories per serving.

Filbert Torte

Let this crunchy nut cake finalize dinner along with sliced winter pears or big strawberries to eat out-of-hand.

1 cup filberts or almonds
1 teaspoon baking powder
8 eggs, separated
⅛ teaspoon each salt and cream of tartar
¾ cup sugar
1 teaspoon grated lemon peel
½ teaspoon almond extract
1/3 cup fine bread crumbs

Grind nuts in a blender until fine. Mix in baking powder. Beat egg whites until foamy, add salt and cream of tartar, and beat until soft peaks form. Beat in ¼ cup of the sugar. Beat yolks until thick and lemon-colored and beat in remaining sugar, lemon peel, almond extract, and crumbs. Stir in nuts and fold in egg whites. Turn into a buttered 10-inch springform pan or a 9-by-13-inch baking pan. Bake in a 350° oven for 30 to 35 minutes, or until the top springs back. Let cool on a rack. Cut round cake into wedges (it makes 18, at 120 calories per serving) or cut rectangular cake into diamonds (it makes 36, at 60 calories per serving). Makes 1 large cake. Total calories: 2200.

178

Orange Soufflé Omelet

A few violets or daisies from the garden lend a charming note to this soufflé platter.

1 orange
4 eggs, separated
¼ cup sugar
grated peel of 1 orange
1 orange
Violets or daisies, if available

Grate the zest from the orange and set aside. Peel the orange and thinly slice; reserve. Beat egg whites until soft peaks form and beat in 2 tablespoons of the sugar, beating until stiff. Beat the yolks until lemon-colored and beat in remaining sugar. Fold in the whites. Mound soufflé mixture on an oven-proof platter, spreading it with a spatula. Bake in a 425° oven for 10 minutes. Decorate the platter edge with sliced oranges and flowers. Makes 4 servings. Contains about 150 calories per serving.

Almond Dollar Wafers

Each crispy cooky is dollar-size and permeated with almond flavor.

⅓ cup almond paste
2 tablespoons sugar
4 teaspoons all-purpose flour
2 egg whites

Place in a mixing bowl the almond paste, sugar, and flour, and beat until blended. Add egg whites and beat until thick and very smooth.
Line baking sheets with foil or parchment paper and butter foil or paper. Drop batter from a teaspoon and spread into very thin 1½-inch rounds. Bake in a 300° oven for 7 to 8 minutes, or until golden brown on the edges. Remove from foil or paper immediately and let cool on a rack. Makes about 2½ dozen. Contains about 20 calories per wafer.

Orange Crêpes Flambé

Triangular packets of crêpes, bathed in a hot orange sauce, make a regal finale.

16 crêpes: see page 76
2 tablespoons butter
¼ cup sugar
1½ tablespoons lemon juice
1 teaspoon grated lemon peel
¼ cup orange-juice concentrate, thawed and undiluted
2 tablespoons brandy
2 tablespoons toasted sliced almonds or chocolate curls from 1 ounce semi-sweet chocolate
1½ cups strawberries for garnish (optional)

First prepare crêpes. Fold crêpes in half and then in half again, forming triangles; set aside. Place butter, sugar, lemon juice, lemon peel, and orange-juice concentrate in a large frying pan and heat together, stirring, until blended. Arrange crêpes overlapping in the pan and heat through. Warm brandy, ignite, and spoon, flaming, over the crêpes. Place 2 crêpes on each dessert plate and scatter the nuts or chocolate curls over them. Garnish with berries, if desired. Makes 8 servings.
Contains about 125 calories each serving.

Café Borgia

Espresso garnished with an Italian flair provides a captivating
Continental coffee drink.

3 cups hot espresso
⅓ cup heavy cream
1 tablespoon brandy or Cognac
2 or 3 strips orange zest, cut into slivers
semisweet chocolate curls (from ½ ounce chocolate)

Pour warm water into brandy snifters or other suitable glasses to heat
them; then drain. Prepare espresso using a Continental coffee mix or
instant espresso. Pour hot into glasses. Whip cream until stiff and beat
in brandy or cognac. Spoon a mound into each cup and garnish each
with a few slivers orange peel and chocolate curls. Serves 4. Contains
about 80 calories per serving.

Coffee Granita

The Italian coffee ice is a cool drink to serve after a summer meal.

⅔ cup sugar
½ cup water
1½ cups triple-strength coffee or espresso
brandy

Combine sugar and water in a saucepan; bring to a boil and boil 1
minute. Remove from heat and stir in coffee. Pour into a freezer
container and freeze just until firm. Turn into a bowl and chop up
coarsely. Then beat with an electric mixer, starting at low speed and
gradually increasing to high, whipping until very fluffy and triple in
volume. Spoon into a refrigerator container and freeze until solid. To
serve, spoon ice into slender wine glasses and pour a teaspoon of
brandy over each serving. Makes about 1¼ quarts, or 6 servings.
Contains about 75 calories per serving.

The Calorie Counter

Food	Weight in Grams	Approximate Measure	Calories
Almonds, shelled	142	1 cup	850
Apple, raw	150	1 med.	70
Apricots, raw	114	3 apricots	55
dried	150	1 cup (40 halves)	390
Artichokes, cooked	100	1 lg. bud (base and soft end of leaves)	51
Jerusalem, raw	100	4 sm., 1½-inch dia.	70
Asparagus, fresh	60	4 spears	10
pieces	145	1 cup	30
Avocados, whole raw fruit	284	California, 3⅛-in. dia.	370
	454	Florida, 3⅝-in. dia.	390
Bacon, broiled or fried	15	2 slices	90
Bamboo shoots	100	¾ cup	25
Banana, raw	150	1 med.	85
Beans, green, fresh cooked	125	1 cup	30
lima, fresh cooked	160	1 cup	180
Bean sprouts, mung	77	1¾ cup	23
Beef braised or pot-roasted, lean and fat	112	4 oz.	330
hamburger, lean, broiled	112	4 oz.	250

181

Food	Weight in Grams	Approximate Measure	Calories
hamburger, regular, broiled	112	4 oz.	330
roast, rib	112	4 oz.	500
rump or heel round	112	4 oz.	220
steak, round	112	4 oz.	220
sirloin	112	4 oz.	440
Beets, fresh cooked	100	2 whole	30
Beverages			
alcoholic			
beer	360	12 fl. oz.	150
Gin, rum, vodka, whiskey, 90-proof	42	1½ oz.	110
Wines, dessert	103	3½ fl. oz.	140
Wines, table	102	3½ fl. oz.	85
Carbonated water	366	12 fl. oz.	115
Coffee and tea	—	—	0
Cola type	369	12 fl. oz.	145
Ginger ale	366	12 fl. oz.	115
Liqueurs, brandy or Cognac	30	1 brandy glass	73
crème de menthe	20	1 cordial glass	67
Curaçao	20	1 cordial glass	54
Root beer	370	12 fl. oz.	150
Blueberries	140	1 cup	85
Bouillon cubes	4	1 cube, about ½ in.	5
Brazil nuts, shelled	15	4 average	97
Bread, white enriched	23	1 slice	60
whole wheat	23	1 slice	55
French or Italian	454	1 lb. loaf	1315
Broccoli	155	1 cup, cooked	40
Brussels sprouts	155	7 to 8 sprouts	55
Butter	14	1 tablespoon	100
Buttermilk, made from skim milk	245	1 cup	90
Cabbage, shredded, raw	100	1 cup	25
Chinese	100	1 cup	15

Food	Weight in Grams	Approximate Measure	Calories
Cakes, angel	53	1/12 of 10-in. cake	135
pound	30	½-in. slice (3 by 3 in.)	140
sponge	66	1/12 of 10-in. cake	195
Candy: caramel or fudge	28	1 oz.	115
peanut brittle	25	1 piece	110
Cantaloupe, raw	385	½ of 5-in. melon	60
Carrots	50	1 carrot	20
Cashew nuts	135	1 cup	760
Cauliflower, raw	100	1 cup	25
Celery	40	1 stalk	5
Chard, leaves and stalks	100	½ cup cooked	21
Cheese — Swiss, Cheddar, Roquefort, or Blue	28	1 oz.	105
Camembert	28	1 oz.	84
Cottage cheese	225	1 cup	240
Cream cheese	15	1 tablespoon	55
Parmesan	28	1 oz.	110
Ricotta	225	1 cup	400
Cherries, raw sweet	130	1 cup	80
Chicken, fresh, broiled	85	3 oz.	115
Chicory or endive, curly	50	15 to 20 inner leaves	10
Chili sauce	17	1 tablespoon	20
Chocolate, bitter or baking	28	1 oz.	145
semisweet, small pieces	170	1 cup	860
Clams, raw	85	3 oz.	65
canned, solids and liquid	85	3 oz.	45
Coconut, fresh	97	1 cup, shredded	335
dried, sweetened	62	1 cup, shredded	340
Cookies, plain and assorted	25	1 cookie, 3-in. dia.	120
Corn	140	1 ear, 5 in. long	70
Cornstarch	8	1 tablespoon	29
Crabmeat, canned	85	3 oz.	85
Crackers, graham	28	4 squares	110
saltines	11	4 squares	50

Food	Weight in Grams	Approximate Measure	Calories
Cream, half-and-half	15	1 tablespoon	20
heavy or whipping	15	1 tablespoon	50
sour	15	1 tablespoon	50
sour half-and-half	15	1 tablespoon	30
Cucumber	207	12 in. by 7 in.	30
Dandelion greens, cooked	90	½ cup	40
Dates	178	1 cup	490
Eggplant	100	2 slices or ½ cup	24
Eggs	50	1 med.	80
egg white	33	1 white	15
egg yolk	17	1 yolk	60
Fats, cooking, vegetable	12.5	1 tablespoon	110
Figs, dried	21	1 fig	60
Filberts	15	10 to 12 nuts	95
Flour, enriched	100	⅞ cup	350
whole wheat	100	¾ cup	333
Gelatin, plain dry powder	7	1 envelope	25
Gooseberries, raw	100	⅔ cup	39
Grapefruit, raw, white	241	½ grapefruit, 3¾-in. dia.	45
raw, pink	241	½ grapefruit, 3¾-in. dia.	50
juice, fresh	246	1 cup	45
Grape juice, canned or bottled	246	1 cup	165
Grapes, raw Concord, Niagara	153	1 cup	65
Muscat, Thompson, Tokay	160	1 cup	95
Honey	21	1 tablespoon	65
Ice cream, regular (10% fat)	133	1 cup	255
rich (approx. 16% fat)	148	1 cup	330
Ice milk, hardened	131	1 cup	200
soft-serve	175	1 cup	265
Jams, preserves, jellies	20	1 tablespoon	55
Lamb, chop, broiled	137	1 chop, 4¼-in. dia.	400
leg, roasted, lean and fat	112	4 oz.	305
lean only	64	2.3 oz.	130

Food	Weight in Grams	Approximate Measure	Calories
Leeks	100	3 or 4, 5 in. long	40
Lemon	106	1 med.	20
juice (or lime juice), fresh	15	1 tablespoon	5
Lentils	95	½ cup, cooked	100
Lettuce, iceberg	464	1 head, 4¼-in. dia.	60
leaves	50	2 lg. leaves	10
Liver, beef, raw	100	2 slices	136
calf, raw	100	2 slices	141
chicken, raw	100	2 large	140
Lobster, canned	85	½ cup	75
Macadamia nuts	15	8 to 12	108
Mangoes	100	1 sm.	60
Margarine, regular	14	1 tablespoon	100
stick (4 sticks to pound)	113	½ cup	815
whipped (6 sticks per pound) stick	76	½ cup	545
Milk, whole	244	1 cup	160
dry, nonfat, instant	70	1 cup	250
low fat, 2%	246	1 cup	145
nonfat, skim	245	1 cup	90
Mushrooms, fresh	100	10 sm. or 4 lg.	16
Nectarines	100	2 med.	60
Oils, salad or cooking, corn, olive, peanut, safflower, or soybean	14	1 tablespoon	125
Olives, green	16	4 med. or 3 extra lg.	15
ripe	10	3 sm. or 2 lg.	15
Onions, raw, yellow	110	1 onion, 2½-in. dia.	40
young green, without tops	50	6 onions	20
Orange, navel	180	1 med.	65
frozen reconstituted	249	1 cup	120
juice, fresh	248	1 cup	110
Oysters, raw	240	1 cup	160
Papayas	182	1 cup, ½-in. cubes	70
Parsley, raw chopped	4	1 tablespoon	trace
Parsnips, cooked	155	1 cup	100

Food	Weight in Grams	Approximate Measure	Calories
Passion fruit	100	½ cup	71
Peaches	114	1 peach, 2-in. dia.	35
Peanut butter	16	1 tablespoon	95
Peanuts, roasted, salted, halves	144	1 cup	840
Pears, raw	182	1 med. pear	100
Peas, edible pod	100	29 to 33 pods	31
green, fresh cooked	160	1 cup	115
Peppers, green, raw	62	1 med.	15
Persimmons	100	1 med.	78
Pickles, dill	135	1 pickle, 4 in. long	15
sweet	20	1 pickle, 2¾ in. long	30
Pie, apple or cherry	135	1/7 of 9-in. pie	350
pecan	118	1/7 of 9-in. pie	490
Pimientos	35	canned, medium	9
Pineapple, raw	140	1 cup, diced	75
canned, syrup pack	260	1 cup, crushed	195
juice, canned	249	1 cup	135
sliced	122	1 lg. slice	135
Pine nuts (pignolias)	15	¼ cup, scant	85
Pistachio nuts	15	30 nuts	88
Pizza, cheese	75	5½-in. sector	185
Plums, raw	60	1 plum	25
Pork, chop	98	1 chop, 3.5 oz.	260
ham, cured	112	4 oz.	325
roast, lean and fat	112	4 oz.	410
Potatoes, baked	99	1 med.	90
Prunes, dried	25	3 med.	67
juice, canned or bottled	256	1 cup	200
Pumpkin, canned	228	1 cup	75
Radishes	40	4 sm.	5
Raisins, seedless	160	1 cup	460
Raspberries, raw	123	1 cup	70
frozen, 10-oz. carton	284	1 carton	275

Food	Weight in Grams	Approximate Measure	Calories
Rhubarb, cooked, sugar added	272	1 cup	385
Rice, white, cooked	168	1 cup	185
Salad dressings, french	16	1 tablespoon	65
Mayonnaise	14	1 tablespoon	100
Salmon, fresh	95	4 oz.	291
smoked	50	2 to 3 slices	89
Sauerkraut, canned	235	1 cup	45
Sausage, bologna	26	2 slices	80
braunschweiger	20	2 slices	80
frankfurter	51	1 frankfurter	155
salami, dry	28	1 oz.	130
Scallops	100	2 or 3	78
Sherbet, orange	193	1 cup	260
Shrimp	112	4 oz.	135
Sole, turbot, red snapper	100	3-by-3-by-⅞-in. piece	156
Soybeans, dried, whole	100	½ cup, dry	331
curd	100	1 cake, 2½ by 2½ by 1 in.	71
Spinach, cooked	180	1 cup	40
Squash, cooked summer	210	1 cup	30
winter	205	1 cup	130
Strawberries, raw	149	1 cup	55
Sugar, brown	14	1 tablespoon	50
white, granulated	12	1 tablespoon	45
white, powdered	8	1 tablespoon	30
Sweet potatoes, baked	110	1 med.	155
Tangerine	114	1 med.	40
Tomato, raw	200	1 med.	40
juice	243	1 cup	45
ketchup	15	1 tablespoon	15
Tuna, canned in oil, drained	85	4 oz.	230
Turkey, roasted	100	3 slices	200
Turnips	155	1 cup	35

Food	Weight in Grams	Approximate Measure	Calories
Veal, cutlet	112	4 oz.	225
roast (lean and fat)	112	4 oz.	305
Vinegar	15	1 tablespoon	trace
Walnuts, black or English chopped	126	1 cup	790
Water chestnuts	25	4 chestnuts	17
Watercress	10	10 sprigs	2
Watermelon, raw	925	1 wedge, 4 by 8 in.	115
Yogurt, made from partially skimmed milk	245	1 cup	125
made from whole milk	245	1 cup	150 to 160

Data from *Nutritive Value of Foods*, Home and Garden Bull. No. 72 revised (Washington, D.C.: U.S. Dept. Agr., 1971) and certain items from "Food Values of Portions Commonly Used," Bowes and Church, 9th ed., Lippincott, Philadelphia.

Daily Energy Allowances

Recommended Amounts for Different Ages and Sexes

	Years (up to)	Weight		Height		Energy in Calories
Infants	.0 to .5	6 kg.	14 lb.	60 cm.	24 in.	kg × 117
	.5 to 1	9	20	71	28	kg × 108
Children	1 to 3	13	28	86	34	1300
	4 to 6	20	44	110	44	1800
	7 to 10	30	66	135	54	2400
Males	11 to 14	44	97	158	63	2800
	15 to 18	61	134	172	69	3000
	19 to 22	67	147	172	69	3000
	23 to 50	70	154	172	69	2700
	51+	70	154	172	69	2400
Females	11 to 14	44	97	155	62	2400
	15 to 18	54	119	162	65	2100
	19 to 22	58	128	162	65	2100
	23 to 50	58	128	162	65	2000
	51+	58	128	162	65	1800
Pregnant						+300
Lactating						+500

From *Recommended Daily Dietary Allowances, Eighth Edition*, Natl. Acad. Sci.-Natl. Research Council Publ. No. 2216 (Washington, D.C.: Natl. Research Council, 1974).

Index

Note: Bold page numbers represent recipes
listed in Ethnic Menus